MACAT

An Analysis of

N. T. Wright's

The New Testament and the People of God

T0344050

Benjamin Laird

ROUTLEDGE

Published by Macat International Ltd
24:13 Coda Centre, 189 Munster Road, London SW6 6AW.

Distributed exclusively by Routledge
2 Park Square, Milton Park, Abingdon, Oxon OX14 4RN
711 Third Avenue, New York, NY 10017, USA

Routledge is an imprint of the Taylor & Francis Group, an informa business

Copyright © 2017 by Macat International Ltd
Macat International has asserted its right under the Copyright, Designs and Patents Act
1988 to be identified as the copyright holder of this work.

The print publication is protected by copyright. Prior to any prohibited reproduction, storage in
a retrieval system, distribution or transmission in any form or by any means, electronic, me-
chanical, recording or otherwise, permission should be obtained from the publisher or where
applicable a license permitting restricted copying in the United Kingdom should be obtained
from the Copyright Licensing Agency Ltd, Barnard's Inn, 86 Fetter Lane, London EC4A 1EN, UK.

The ePublication is protected by copyright and must not be copied, reproduced, transferred,
distributed, leased, licensed or publicly performed or used in any way except as specifically
permitted in writing by the publishers, as allowed under the terms and conditions under which
it was purchased, or as strictly permitted by applicable copyright law. Any unauthorised distribution or use of this text may be a direct infringement of the authors and the publishers' rights
and those responsible may be liable in law accordingly.

www.macat.com
info@macat.com

Cataloguing in Publication Data
A catalogue record for this book is available from the British Library.
Library of Congress Cataloguing-in-Publication Data is available upon request.
Cover illustration: Capucine Deslouis

ISBN 978-1-912453-84-9 (hardback)
ISBN 978-1-912453-66-5 (paperback)
ISBN 978-1-912453-72-6 (e-book)

Printed and bound by CPI Group (UK) Ltd, Croydon, CR0 4YY

Notice
The information in this book is designed to orientate readers of the work under analysis,
to elucidate and contextualise its key ideas and themes, and to aid in the development
of critical thinking skills. It is not meant to be used, nor should it be used, as a
substitute for original thinking or in place of original writing or research. References and
notes are provided for informational purposes and their presence does not constitute
endorsement of the information or opinions therein. This book is presented solely for
educational purposes. It is sold on the understanding that the publisher is not engaged
to provide any scholarly advice. The publisher has made every effort to ensure that
this book is accurate and up-to-date, but makes no warranties or representations with
regard to the completeness or reliability of the information it contains. The information
and the opinions provided herein are not guaranteed or warranted to produce particular
results and may not be suitable for students of every ability. The publisher shall not be
liable for any loss, damage or disruption arising from any errors or omissions, or from
the use of this book, including, but not limited to, special, incidental, consequential or
other damages caused, or alleged to have been caused, directly or indirectly, by the
information contained within.

CONTENTS

THE MACAT LIBRARY

The Macat Library is a series of unique academic explorations of seminal works in the humanities and social sciences – books and papers that have had a significant and widely recognised impact on their disciplines. It has been created to serve as much more than just a summary of what lies between the covers of a great book. It illuminates and explores the influences on, ideas of, and impact of that book. Our goal is to offer a learning resource that encourages critical thinking and fosters a better, deeper understanding of important ideas.

Each publication is divided into three Sections: Influences, Ideas, and Impact. Each Section has four Modules. These explore every important facet of the work, and the responses to it.

This Section-Module structure makes a Macat Library book easy to use, but it has another important feature. Because each Macat book is written to the same format, it is possible (and encouraged!) to cross-reference multiple Macat books along the same lines of inquiry or research. This allows the reader to open up interesting interdisciplinary pathways.

To further aid your reading, lists of glossary terms and people mentioned are included at the end of this book (these are indicated by an asterisk [*] throughout) – as well as a list of works cited.

Macat has worked with the University of Cambridge to identify the elements of critical thinking and understand the ways in which six different skills combine to enable effective thinking.
Three allow us to fully understand a problem; three more give us the tools to solve it. Together, these six skills make up the **PACIER** model of critical thinking. They are:

ANALYSIS – understanding how an argument is built
EVALUATION – exploring the strengths and weaknesses of an argument
INTERPRETATION – understanding issues of meaning

CREATIVE THINKING – coming up with new ideas and fresh connections
PROBLEM-SOLVING – producing strong solutions
REASONING – creating strong arguments

To find out more, visit **WWW.MACAT.COM.**

CRITICAL THINKING AND *THE NEW TESTAMENT AND THE PEOPLE OF GOD*

Primary Critical Thinking Skill: EVALUATION
Secondary Critical Thinking Skill: CREATIVE THINKING

The scholarly works of N.T. Wright demonstrate the effective evaluation skills that are necessary when dealing with ancient texts and complicated theological subjects. In *The New Testament and the People of God*, Wright exhibits not only his comprehensive knowledge of the primary sources that are of relevance to the study of early Christianity, but also his ability to interpret these writings in light of their ancient historical and cultural contexts. Wright's evaluation of numerous ancient sources serves as a model of determining not just what a text says, but how it should be understood and interpreted in light of its wider contexts.

In addition to his astute and perceptive evaluation of a wide range of ancient and modern sources, Wright is well known for his ability to add fresh insights to subjects that have already received significant scholarly attention, in his case subjects such as the theology of the Apostle Paul or the beliefs of early Christians. His creative thinking skills are exemplified not only in the numerous illustrations, analogies, and examples that are used to explain difficult concepts, but in his ability to produce novel explanations for evidence that has existed—and been combed over—for centuries.

ABOUT THE AUTHOR OF THE ORIGINAL WORK

Widely regarded as one of today's foremost New Testament scholars, **N. T. Wright** serves as Research Professor of New Testament and Early Christianity at the University of Saint Andrews in Scotland. Born in Morpeth, England in 1948, Wright has written dozens of scholarly works on various New Testament subjects as well as several theological works written for a popular audience. He has also served the Anglican Church in various capacities, most recently as the Bishop of Durham.

ABOUT THE AUTHOR OF THE ANALYSIS

A native of Denver, Colorado, **Benjamin Laird** currently serves as Assistant Professor of Biblical Studies at Liberty University in Lynchburg, VA. His PhD research from University of Aberdeen examined the collection, publication, and early circulation of the Apostle Paul's writings in early Christianity.

ABOUT MACAT

GREAT WORKS FOR CRITICAL THINKING

Macat is focused on making the ideas of the world's great thinkers accessible and comprehensible to everybody, everywhere, in ways that promote the development of enhanced critical thinking skills.

It works with leading academics from the world's top universities to produce new analyses that focus on the ideas and the impact of the most influential works ever written across a wide variety of academic disciplines. Each of the works that sit at the heart of its growing library is an enduring example of great thinking. But by setting them in context – and looking at the influences that shaped their authors, as well as the responses they provoked – Macat encourages readers to look at these classics and game-changers with fresh eyes. Readers learn to think, engage and challenge their ideas, rather than simply accepting them.

'Macat offers an amazing first-of-its-kind tool for interdisciplinary learning and research. Its focus on works that transformed their disciplines and its rigorous approach, drawing on the world's leading experts and educational institutions, opens up a world-class education to anyone.'

Andreas Schleicher
Director for Education and Skills, Organisation for Economic Co-operation and Development

'Macat is taking on some of the major challenges in university education ... They have drawn together a strong team of active academics who are producing teaching materials that are novel in the breadth of their approach.'

Prof Lord Broers,
former Vice-Chancellor of the University of Cambridge

'The Macat vision is exceptionally exciting. It focuses upon new modes of learning which analyse and explain seminal texts which have profoundly influenced world thinking and so social and economic development. It promotes the kind of critical thinking which is essential for any society and economy. This is the learning of the future.'

Rt Hon Charles Clarke, former UK Secretary of State for Education

'The Macat analyses provide immediate access to the critical conversation surrounding the books that have shaped their respective discipline, which will make them an invaluable resource to all of those, students and teachers, working in the field.'

Professor William Tronzo, University of California at San Diego

WAYS IN TO THE TEXT

KEY POINTS

- N. T. Wright is a leading British New Testament scholar and a former Bishop of Durham.

- He argues that modern readers cannot appreciate the message of the New Testament without understanding the beliefs of first-century Jews.

- *The New Testament and the People of God* surveys the key beliefs of early Jews and the degree to which the first Christians shared them.

Who is Nicholas Thomas Wright?

Born in Morpeth, England in 1941, Nicholas Thomas Wright—often referred to simply as N. T. Wright—is the author of *The New Testament and the People of God* and widely regarded as one of the foremost contemporary New Testament* scholars and theologians. Although his works cover a wide range of subjects, he has become known principally for his work on Jesus,* the Gospels,* and the Apostle Paul.* Since completing his doctorate at Oxford in 1981 under the supervision of George Caird,* Wright has taught at a number of universities, such as McGill University in Montreal, Canada, Oxford University, and since 2010 at the University of St. Andrews in Scotland. Before completing his doctoral studies, he served as a tutor at Oxford and Cambridge. In addition to his writing and teaching, Wright is a frequent speaker at academic conferences and other events.

Wright has also served as a clergyman, most notably as Bishop of Durham from 2003 to 2010. He was also the Dean of Lichfield from 1994 to 1999, and Canon Theologian of Westminster from 2000 to 2003. His involvement in the Anglican Church* has widened the target audience of many of his published works. Much of Wright's work was written chiefly for the academic community. However, he has also written the *New Testament for Everyone* series, a collection of commentaries on the books of the New Testament aimed at a more general readership. As a result, he has accumulated an unusually broad following

What does *The New Testament and the People of God* say?

For centuries, Christianity and Judaism have been widely regarded as two separate systems of religious thought and practice. While the two traditions share a common history as well as some common beliefs, the differences between the two are also significant and the history of the last 2,000 years has strengthened these perceived differences. Without dismissing the unique features of either religion, N.T. Wright argues that if you want to understand Christian theology, you must also understand the world of first-century Judaism and how Jesus and the earliest Christians understood their faith in relation to the common beliefs of their time. On this basis, Wright offers a thorough investigation of several of the core theological beliefs of first-century Jews and how they relate to the founding beliefs of Christianity. As Wright wrote, "Far from being mutually isolated, Christianity and Judaism were, for the first generation at least, intertwined in ways that must at the time have seemed quite inextricable."[1]

Wright's contention that Christian theology must be built upon a proper understanding of the eschatological* expectations and theological beliefs of Jews living in the first century is one of the book's most important features. While not all scholars agree with Wright's historical observations, not least the manner in which he articulates the theological beliefs of first-century Jews, his call to bridge the divide between Christian theology and its Jewish heritage has been widely embraced. Regardless of one's perspective of Wright's conclusions, *The New Testament and the People of God* is now regarded as a seminal work of significant importance.[2] As scholar A.K.M. Adam* has described it, "Few have equaled Wright's historical overview of first-century Judaism and the genesis of Christianity. Those who disagree with Wright will have to outweigh his copious evidence arrayed in powerful arguments, and all scholars will have to position themselves with relation to him."[3]

Wright went on to challenge the traditional understanding of several passages of the New Testament, many of them in the Pauline Epistles.* Much of his later work is based on his contention that first-century Jews understood themselves to be part of a covenantal* community. This meant that obedience to Mosaic Law* was regarded not as the means by which individuals entered into the community but simply as the expectation of those who are already part of the community.

Why does *The New Testament and the People of God* matter?

Wright thinks that to interpret the New Testament properly, especially the mission of Jesus as understood by the four Gospel writers, modern interpreters must also understand the world of the first century and, in particular, the Jewish beliefs of the time and how they related to the early Christian faith. These topics are treated thoroughly and with great clarity in his book.[4] Among the many topics Wright addresses is the eschatological hopes and expectations of Jews in the first century. Contrary to several previous scholars, he argues that the majority did not anticipate that the physical world would soon be destroyed in some kind of cataclysmic event coinciding with the return of the awaited Messiah.* He contends, rather, that the expectation was for a renewed earth but one without the many troubles of the day. This hope, Wright suggests, would have been especially fitting for Jews in the first century living under the yoke of the Roman Empire* who had already endured several centuries of oppression from foreign powers. While not all readers will agree with all of Wright's conclusions, the background information he provides regarding the religious thought of the Jews and Christians in the first century is of great importance.

Wright paints a detailed picture of the Greco-Roman world, and the book is also a helpful model showing how interpreters might engage in the scholarly synthesis of multiple fields of study. Wright's in-depth historical investigation is coupled with thoughtful theological analysis and a consideration of various philosophical questions. In an age when many scholars tend to specialize in a very specific field of study and rarely venture outside their single area of expertise, Wright has demonstrated how the scholarly exploration of multiple fields of study can greatly enrich one's research. For those interested specifically in the field of New Testament studies, *The New Testament and the People of God* is of significant relevance given Wright's ability to carefully ground his theological conclusions on a solid historical foundation.

NOTES

1   N.T. Wright, *The New Testament and the People of God* (Minneapolis, Minn.: Fortress Press, 1992), 467-468.

2   N.T. Wright, *The New Testament and the People of God* (Minneapolis, Minn.: Fortress Press, 1992).

3   A.K.M. Adam, Book Review of *The New Testament and the People of God*. Catholic Biblical Quarterly 56 (1994): 166.

4   See, especially, Wright, *New Testament*, 147-336.

SECTION 1
INFLUENCES

MODULE 1
THE AUTHOR AND THE
HISTORICAL CONTEXT

KEY POINTS

- *The New Testament and the People of God* serves as an introduction to a longer series, providing an overview of the major beliefs of first-century Jews.

- Wright has spent his entire career as a biblical scholar and clergyman in the Anglican Church.

- A central concern of Wright is correcting what he believes to be erroneous teachings about Christian theology that have been perpetuated since the Protestant Reformation.

Why Read This Text?

N. T. Wright's *The New Testament and the People of God* makes several significant contributions to the field of New Testament studies. Firstly, it serves as an introduction to Wright's *Christian Origins and the Question of God* series and provides a helpful framework for reading the remaining volumes.[1] While each of the volumes in the series may be read on its own, in this book, Wright provides a thorough investigation into several foundational matters that play a role in the subsequent volumes. He provides a substantial explanation, for example, of his hermeneutical* approach and methodology.

Secondly, the book's fresh and substantive examination of the nature of first-century Judaism has challenged longstanding assumptions about the theology of the Apostle Paul.[2] Before the publications of New Testament scholars such as Wright, James Dunn,* and E.P. Sanders,* few had analyzed the relevant ancient primary sources to any significant degree. Moreover, no one had

> **❝** Nicholas Tom Wright ... is a remarkable blend of weighty academic scholarship, ecclesiastical leadership, ecumenical involvement, prophetic social engagement, popular Christian advocacy, musical talent, and family commitment. **❞**
>
> John Piper, *The Future of Justification: A Response to N. T. Wright*

investigated the common political and religious assumptions of first-century Jews and how they were likely to have been shared by the writers of the New Testament.

Thirdly, Wright shows his readers how the world view and major religious beliefs of first-century Jews would have affected the theological perspectives of the New Testament authors. While numerous works have been published in recent decades about the social, religious, and political world of first-century Judaism, few have offered such a thorough challenge to the prevailing view of the interpretation of the New Testament in light of these findings. Wright is a careful historian, but his primary motivation is to put himself in a position to do the work of a theologian more skillfully and accurately.

Author's Life

Wright was born in Morpeth, England in 1941. He is a biblical scholar and ordained clergyman in the Anglican Church who, since 2010, has served as Professor of New Testament and Early Christianity at the University of Saint Andrews, in Scotland. Wright received his academic training at the University of Oxford where he earned BA, MA, DD, and D Phil degrees. Following the completing of his doctoral studies in 1981, he taught at McGill University in Montreal, Canada from 1981 to 1986, and then at the University of Oxford from 1986 to 1993 and again from 1999 to 2000.[3]

In addition to his academic career, Wright has served in a variety of leadership roles within the Anglican Church. Following his tenure at McGill University, Wright relocated to England to serve as the Dean of Lichfield Cathedral, a post which he held from 1994 to 1999. He was Canon Theologian of Westminster Abbey* from 2000 to 2003, and, most recently, was Bishop of Durham from 2003 to 2010. While Wright does not currently serve the Anglican Church in an official capacity, he remains a frequent speaker at various churches and assemblies and continues to remain an active participant in the life of the church.

Wright is perhaps best known for his many writings. While many of his publications were written for an academic readership, he has written several more popular works, such as the *Bible for Everyone* series. Over the years, Wright has sometimes spoken out on matters of contemporary debate, such as the 2003 Iraq war and, more directly related to the contemporary Anglican Church, the controversy surrounding the ordination of women, and the subject of homosexuality.[4]

Author's Background

Wright wrote *The New Testament and the People of God* while he was a lecturer in New Testament at Oxford University. As he noted in his preface, an initial draft was produced in Jerusalem during a sabbatical from teaching. The book contains Wright's mature reflections on a number of very complicated subjects relating to hermeneutical theory, the socio-political context of the first century, and the major beliefs of first-century Jews and early Christians. The work is not a reaction to any particular event that took place during his lifetime, but is the product of many years of scholarly investigation.

This is not to say, however, that the volume was in no respect the product of its time or that Wright was uninterested in responding to the prevailing thought. He certainly built upon scholarship pertaining to Second Temple Judaism* and engaged with several primary sources from this period that had only recently been discovered. Wright was particularly concerned with correcting various interpretations of the New Testament that he observed had been prevalent since the Protestant Reformation.* Although Wright positions himself within the Reformed Protestant tradition, he contends that several of the leaders of the Reformation and those who have followed them have often attempted to understand the writings of the New Testament without giving consideration to the key theological beliefs of first-century Jews. Since the Reformation, for example, it has generally been assumed that first-century Judaism was essentially a religion that taught that salvation might be obtained by following the many laws found in the Hebrew Torah.* Wright vigorously challenges this idea. Much of the research in this book and many of his subsequent publications leads to the alternative conclusion that first-century Jews observed the Torah not as a means of salvation but in response to their covenantal relationship to God.

NOTES

1   For a discussion on the origin of the series, see Wright, *New Testament*, xv.

2   See, especially, Wright, *New Testament*, 145-338.

3   For more biographical information on the life of Wright, see Alastair Roberts, "N.T. Wright: A Biography," *Alastair's Adversaria*, accessed January 18, 2018,   https://alastairadversaria.com/2006/09/11/nt-wright-a-biography/

4   Wright has been supportive of the ordination of women in the Anglican Church and opposed to homosexual marriage and the ordination of openly gay clergy.

MODULE 2
ACADEMIC CONTEXT

KEY POINTS

- Wright seeks to provide a more historically credible understanding of the theological perspectives of the authors of the New Testament.

- Much of his academic research has been built upon the previous works of Krister Stendahl and E.P. Sanders.

- George Caird, C.S. Lewis, and T.S. Eliot have been especially influential on Wright's work.

The Work in its Context

N. T. Wright, author of *The New Testament and the People of God*, is widely acclaimed for his scholarly contributions in a number of academic disciplines. In addition to his expertise in Christian theology and hermeneutics, he is well regarded as an historian and biblical scholar. His academic writings address a variety of topics and demonstrate his ability to synthesize research in multiple fields, particularly Second Temple Judaism,* early Christianity, and theology. As he has often contended, it is difficult to engage in meaningful theological work without also engaging in the work of an historian. Equally, it is difficult to evaluate the first-century setting of the New Testament writings without also considering the theology and worldview of the people of that time.

Wright's writing career may be regarded as an attempt to bridge the divide between historical inquiry and theological studies in the academic world. Although he has written on a number of subjects relating both to the theology and the historical background of the New Testament, much of his research has focused on early Christian

> **❝** On the one hand, studying the theology of the New Testament depends on some belief, however vague, that certain things that happened in the first century are in some sense normative or authoritative for subsequent Christianity. On the other hand, studying the history of early Christianity is impossible without a clear grasp of early Christian beliefs. **❞**
>
> Wright, *The New Testament and the People of God*, 13

beliefs and the historical and religious environment of New Testament times. Wright's literary career emerged at a time when a small number of New Testament scholars were first beginning to reconsider some important assumptions in the interpretation of the New Testament, most notably, the doctrine of justification and the eschatological outlook of Jews in the first century. As Wright and others have suggested, misperceptions and faulty conclusions concerning first-century Jewish beliefs have resulted in several erroneous conclusions about the particular theological beliefs of Jesus and the early Christians.

Overview of the Field

One of Wright's central concerns is that the New Testament is often approached with an inappropriate set of questions and misguided concerns that do not reflect the interests of its authors. Wright, is not the first scholar to raise such concerns. In a somewhat obscure article written in 1963, the Swedish biblical scholar Krister Stendahl* raised the concern that the writings of the Apostle Paul have been interpreted from a Western point of view that does not take Paul's Jewish background into account.[1] Stendahl's work did not offer a thorough examination of Second Temple Judaism, but it did draw attention to what he considered a disconnect between historical studies of the background of the New Testament writings and biblical interpretation.

Another influential scholarly work that appeared before *The New Testament and the People of God* was *Paul and Palestinian Judaism*,[2] by E.P. Sanders, published in 1977. Sanders's work was ground breaking in that it challenged common assumptions about the religious thought of first-century Jews, especially how they viewed the relationship between salvation and the observance of the Torah.

Sanders's view, which he referred to as "Covenantal Nomism,"* argues that first-century Judaism did not advocate a system of salvation by works, that is, the belief that individuals must perform good deeds and follow various commandments in order to experience salvation. Instead, first-century Jews advocated the observance of the Mosaic Law, in response to their covenantal relationship to God. The implications of this theory are far reaching for the study of the New Testament's teaching relating to the doctrine of salvation in general, and Paul's teaching regarding justification in particular.

Academic Influences

Wright has interacted with many scholars throughout his career but he acknowledges a few as influences. He completed his doctoral work under the supervision of George Caird, a long-time biblical scholar at the University of Oxford who exposed Wright to many of the primary sources needed for an understanding of the political, religious and social world of first-century Israel. In addition to his interest in New Testament eschatology,* the historical Jesus and Paul, Caird also addressed more political subjects such as the place of women in society and the church, the ethics of war, and racism.

In addition to his former doctoral supervisor, Wright mentions two particular English authors as influences on his writing and/or perspective on theological matters early in his career.[3] The first was the C.S. Lewis,* the British writer and theologian known primarily today for *The Chronicles of Narnia*, and other works such as *Mere*

Christianity and *The Screwtape Letters.* While Wright sometimes disagrees with him on theological matters, he has acknowledged that Lewis was one of the first to challenge his thinking regarding the reality of the Bible's claims and its implications for modern Christianity.

Finally, Wright has pointed to the British poet T.S. Eliot* as an early influence on his writing, praising the depth and richness of his many poems and plays and, in particular, *Four Quartets,* one of Eliot's best-known works, a series of four poems written over a six year period. As Wright reflects, this work is about Eliot "coming back to Christian faith as a resolution of all of the questions that he's had all

NOTES

1   Krister Stendahl, "The Apostle Paul and the Introspective Conscience of the West," *Harvard Theological Review* 56, no. 3 (1963): 199–215.

2   E.P. Sanders, *Paul and Palestinian Judaism: A Comparison of Patterns of Religion* (Minneapolis, Minn.: Fortress Press, 1977). Sanders's next book was *Paul, the Law, and the Jewish People* (Minneapolis, Minn.: Fortress Press, 1983).

3   Krish Kandiah, "Three Books That Changed NT Wright's Life," *Christianity Today,* accessed January 2, 2018, https://www.christiantoday.com/article/three-books-that-changed-nt-wrights-life/104297.htm.

4   Kandiah, "Three Books."

MODULE 3
THE PROBLEM

KEY POINTS

- Wright attempts to identify the main theological questions and concerns of the New Testament authors.

- Many of the themes that he takes u were previously addressed by Krister Stendahl and E.P. Sanders.

- Wright, along with Sanders and James Dunn, has defended the New Perspective on Paul, though not all scholars are convinced of its merit.

Core Question

Throughout *The New Testament and the People of God*, N. T. Wright argues that, when interpreting the New Testament writings, it is important to consider the extent to which the early Christians shared the common beliefs of first-century Jews. Nearly all of the New Testament writers came from a Jewish background, so Wright argues that it is essential to have an informed understanding of Jewish beliefs and particularly how they thought God would intervene to deliver them from their adversaries.

Given this concern, perhaps the single most important question that Wright and other scholars have asked was how the first Christians, especially the writers of the New Testament, believed God had fulfilled his promises to Abraham.* Modern readers often approach the Bible with questions and concerns relating to their individual faith. Wright and others have argued, however, that the overarching concerns of the first Christians and the authors of the New Testament were broader. In particular, they were related to

> ❝ We need to advance some hypotheses about the historical situation within which the New Testament writings were born. This will involve a historical reconstruction of the Judaism and Christianity of the first century. We know a good deal more about ancient Judaism than we used to, and I shall draw on this new knowledge in some detail. ❞
>
> Wright, *The New Testament and the People of God*, 27

God's involvement in human history and the implications of the coming of Jesus Christ and his subsequent death and resurrection.

Did the work of Christ transform how God's people relate to the stipulations of the Torah? Did Christ usher in a new phase of human history in which God relates to his people in different ways? Given the continued presence of evil and oppression in the world, how are we to understand God's plan to bring peace on earth? These and other related questions were beginning to be asked with greater rigor at the time Wright published *The New Testament and the People of God*, a work which interacts extensively with many relevant primary resources from early Christianity and Second Temple Judaism.

The Participants

Although Wright is one of the better known scholars to examine primary literature from the Second Temple period, he is certainly not the only one who has embarked on this task. Two scholars in particular laid the foundations for several of the ideas taken up later by Wright.

The Swedish biblical scholar Krister Stendahl was one of the first academics to contend that the our understanding of the Apostle Paul's writings has been influenced by modern questions about personal faith rather than the original concerns of Paul.[1] In other words,

Stendahl was persuaded that modern readers have often failed to identify Paul's own objectives in his writings and that this failure has resulted in a somewhat distorted understanding of his message. As a result of the influence of Augustine of Hippo's* *Confessions*, a work that places a significant emphasis on personal guilt and repentance, as well as the decline of Jewish influence on the Christian faith, Stendahl concluded that questions common to early Jewish Christians had been replaced with questions relating to personal faith.

Many of the themes taken up by Wright were previously explored in E.P. Sanders's landmark book *Paul and Palestinian Judaism*.[2] Sanders was one of the first to question the traditional understanding of first-century Judaism and to explore how common misunderstandings about it may have misled biblical scholars in their attempt to understand Paul. Wright took up many of the same themes as Sanders, but has often reached different conclusions about Paul's understanding of the Mosaic Law and the doctrine of justification. Throughout his career, Wright has sought to bring clarity to this subject through a number of writings on Paul and first-century Judaism.[3]

The Contemporary Debate

Wright's work has received an enormous amount of scholarly attention in recent decades. Several biblical scholars have adopted his viewpoints regarding the nature of first-century Judaism and the beliefs of early Christians, and many scholars have engaged in scholarly work that relates to the major themes addressed in *The New Testament and the People of God*.

In addition to Stendahl and Sanders—and the latter remains active in scholarly research[4]—a number of contemporary scholars have identified themselves as supporters of the so-called New Perspective on Paul.* The term was coined by James Dunn, Emeritus Lightfoot Professor of Divinity at the University of Durham and he has become, along with Wright, a major proponent and leading figure within the movement. While there is not complete consensus among all the scholars who advocate the New Perspective, they have largely agreed that Christian theologians and biblical scholars have fundamentally misunderstood the nature of first-century Judaism. These misunderstandings, proponents of the New Perspective argue, have often resulted in a misreading of key passages relating to Paul's understanding of Judaism, the Mosaic Law, and the doctrine of justification. Wright, Dunn, Sanders, and others have insisted, for example, that Martin Luther,* the influential Protestant Reformer, interpreted the Pauline writings in terms of the religious environment of his own time. So, in his attempt to curtail the works-righteousness model of salvation that was being propagated by the Roman Catholic Church,* Martin Luther interpreted the letters of Paul as if Paul's Jewish opponents also advocated a system of works righteousness. Wright, along with other supporters of the New Perspective on Paul, contends that modern scholars must re-evaluate common assumptions

NOTES

1   See Stendahl, "Paul."

2   Sanders, *Paul and Palestinian Judaism.*

3   Other notable works by Wright in which he discusses his theories relating to Paul and first-century Judaism include *The Climax of the Covenant: Christ and the Law in Pauline Theology* (Minneapolis, Minn.: Fortress Press, 1991); *What St Paul Really Said* (Grand Rapids, Mich.: Eerdmans, 1997); *Paul: Fresh Perspectives* (Minneapolis, Minn.: Fortress Press, 2005); *Justification* (Grand Rapids, Mich.: IVP Academic, 2009); and *Paul and the Faithfulness of God* (Minneapolis, Minn.: Fortress Press, 2013).

4   See, for example, his recently published *Paul: The Apostle's Life, Letters, and Thought.*

MODULE 4
THE AUTHOR'S CONTRIBUTION

KEY POINTS

- *The New Testament and the People of God* is a unique and groundbreaking study and brings new insight into the Jewish background of the New Testament.

- Wright demonstrates how biblical narratives are used to reveal insights about the mission of Jesus and how this relates to God's fulfillment of the promises contained in the Old Testament.

- He argues that the New Testament cannot be fully understood without a grasp of the first-century contexts in which it was written.

Author's Aims

N.T. Wright's *The New Testament and the People of God* is written from the perspective that many attempts to describe the theology of the New Testament are too limited either in terms of the depth of their study or the themes that are explored. As a result, Wright embarked on what he describes as "a full examination of what a contemporary Christian literary, historical, and theological project might look like."[1] Wright discusses in great detail the landscape of first-century social, religious, and political life to enable modern readers to interpret the writings of the New Testament authors and achieve a more nuanced understanding of how they sought to portray the mission of Jesus.

The book introduces the reader to the world of first-century Judaism and lays the foundations for the remaining volumes in the series. The first five chapters–nearly 150 pages–discuss some of the

> **❝ I hope ... to offer a consistent hypothesis on the origin of Christianity, with particular relation to Jesus, Paul and the gospels, which will set out new ways of understanding major movements and thought-patterns, and suggest new lines that exegesis can follow up. ❞**
>
> Wright, *The New Testament and the People of God*, xiv.

ways the New Testament has been interpreted and misunderstood in recent centuries. Wright goes on to emphasize the importance of interpreting first-century Judaism in its proper context. He discusses some of the common features that characterized all Jews and describes in detail the diverse Jewish movements that were influential during the first century and beyond. He discusses such Jewish groups as the Pharisees,* Sadducees* and the Essenes.*[2] as well as some of the characteristics of early Christianity, a movement that was fundamentally and inherently Jewish in nature.

Wright's scholarship is innovative in many ways but his thorough study of the Jewish background of Christianity is perhaps his most important contribution. While Christianity's Jewish roots have been widely acknowledged, few have offered such a comprehensive study of the manner in which the authors of the New Testament were influenced by Jewish traditions and theological beliefs.

Approach

Early in his career N.T.Wright came to the conclusion that for many years scholars had been reading the New Testament, particularly the Gospels and the writings of Paul, without considering the common theological assumptions shared by first-century Jews. This is problematic, Wright argues, because without an awareness of these concerns, anticipations, and assumptions, it is difficult to understand the New Testament's treatment of such important subjects as the place of the Mosaic Law and the doctrines of justification and salvation. A failure to enter into the world of the first century, Wright contends, has caused many scholars and contemporary readers to ask the wrong questions of the New Testament authors or to misunderstand the nature of the subjects they address.

In his thorough discussion of the Jewish background of the New Testament and the relationship of early Christianity to the Jewish faith, Wright offers several fresh perspectives and unique insights. He considers, for example, the use of stories in Jewish traditions and how the various stories in the Gospel accounts are used to express a particular worldview. As Wright contends, the New Testament is "a Jewish book, telling Jewish-style stories, yet telling them for the world. It is a book of the world, retelling the story of the world as the story of Israel, and the story of Israel as the story of Jesus, in order to subvert the world's stories, and to lay before the world the claim of Jesus to be its sovereign."[3] In other words, the many stories about Jesus in the Gospel accounts are there not simply to teach moral lessons or to reveal various aspects of his nature, but to demonstrate the manner in which Jesus was fulfilling God's promises to His people and bringing about a new age in world history.

Contribution in Context

Wright was one of the first modern New Testament scholars to draw attention to the necessity of interpreting the writings of the New Testament from the perspective of its Jewish background. Before the publication of *The New Testament and the People of God*, many studies had explored the Jewish background of the New Testament and even more had considered the message and theology of the New Testament. However, Wright's book brought these two themes together, offering a comprehensive and thorough examination into how the New Testament's Jewish background provides a true insight into its interpretation. Wright agreed with Krister Stendahl's thesis that an understanding of the meaning of the New Testament is difficult to achieve without an appreciation and awareness of common first-century Jewish assumptions, including the place of Israel in world history, the role of the coming Jewish messiah, and the ways in which Jews understood the nature of the Mosaic Law.[4] With this in view, Wright produced a comprehensive study of the Jewish background of the New Testament with the objective of achieving a more precise understanding of its overarching themes.

The book builds on the previous work of E.P. Sanders who, 15 years before the publication of *The New Testament and the People of God*, wrote the seminal work *Paul and Palestinian Judaism*.[5] This was one of the first scholarly studies to challenge prevailing ideas about the nature of first-century Judaism. Wright, in general agreement with Sanders, has written on the subject extensively, offering a sustained and well-developed treatment of how the Jewish background of the New Testament enables the reader to understand more fully several of its most important themes.

NOTES

1   Wright, *New Testament*, 27.

2   For a scholarly treatment of the most influential religious parties in Second Temple Judaism, see Anthony Saldarini and James VanderKam, *Pharisees, Scribes and Sadducees in Palestinian Society* (Grand Rapids, MI.: Eerdmans, 2001).

3   Wright, *New Testament*, 469.

4   Stendahl, "The Apostle Paul."

5   Sanders, *Paul and Palestinian Judaism*.

SECTION 2
IDEAS

MAIN IDEAS

KEY POINTS

- The main theological beliefs of Christianity cannot be fully understood without an examination of their Jewish roots.

- Christianity and Judaism share a common history and a common hope that God will one day bring restoration and healing to the world.

- *The New Testament and the People of God* is written primarily for a scholarly audience.

Key Themes

Although N. T. Wright's *The New Testament and the People of God* explores a variety of subjects and interacts with a number of scholarly disciplines, its main theme is the Jewish nature of early Christianity. Wright argues that early Christianity was inescapably Jewish at its core. The first Christians were Jews who believed that a new age had dawned in which many of the promises in the Hebrew Bible* had been fulfilled in the person and work of Jesus. They understood Jesus to be the Messiah who had come from God to establish a kingdom on earth as promised by God to Abraham and as prophesied by the Old Testament prophets.

Wright contends that modern readers need an informed knowledge of first-century Judaism if they are to understand fully the message of the New Testament. This is the subject of the last two-thirds of his book although he admits that Judaism in the first century was very diverse. There were various sects and divisions even before the destruction of the Jerusalem temple in 70 A.D.,[1] but their differences became even more pronounced afterwards as the Jews attempted to

> ❝ Within fifty years of the death of Jesus ... those who saw themselves as Jesus' followers were claiming that they were the true heirs of the promises made by the creator God to Abraham, Isaac, and Jacob, and that the Jewish Scriptures were to be read in terms of a new fulfilment. ❞
>
> Wright, *The New Testament and the People of God*, 467

grapple with how to move on from such a tragedy. Given these many different views, Wright suggests that it is more proper to speak of "Judaisms" than it is of "Judaism" as though it were a monolithic and static religion. He gives the reader an overview of several notable Jewish sects, such as the Pharisees, Essenes, and Sadducees, and surveys a generous amount of Jewish writings, in particular that of the Jewish historian Josephus.* While the majority of Jews in the first century shared certain characteristics—the desire for liberation being one of them—they differed on other issues such as the role and implementation of the Torah, the proper response to Gentile suppressors,[2] the significance of the temple, the authority and role of tradition, the continuation of the Jewish feasts and sacrifices, and many more.

Wright believes that many Christian interpreters have failed to understand not only the common assumptions shared by first-century Jews, but also the various matters on which they disagreed. This failure, he argues, has resulted at times in a misguided understanding of the New Testament. Wright is largely successful in his effort to explore the various movements within first-century Judaism. He discusses a number of primary sources and assists the reader in deciphering the common assumptions shared by all first-century Jews as well as important matters of disagreement. He notes, for example, that while there were differing perspectives on theological matters, they typically shared a common worldview—one that recognized the restoration of Israel as the culmination of world history. Wright is certainly not the first writer to discuss the nature of first-century Judaism. However, this book is unique in its ability not only to discuss the religious, political and social landscape of first-century Israel, but how this background in turn colours the message of the New Testament.

Exploring the Ideas

In his discussion of the Jewish background of Christianity, Wright explores several unique features of first-century Judaism and its relationship with the nascent Christian movement. With the possible exception of Luke, each of the authors of the New Testament was Jewish by birth and shared many of the common beliefs of other Jews of their time. As Wright notes, the New Testament "is a Jewish book, telling Jewish-style stories, yet telling them for the world. It is a book of the world, retelling the story of the world as the story of Israel, and the story of Israel as the story of Jesus, in order to subvert the world's stories, and to lay before the world the claim of Jesus to be its sovereign."[3]

Given the profound influence of Judaism on early Christianity, Wright believes that Christianity cannot be regarded as an independent movement that is historically and theologically distinct from Judaism. As he observes, both religions share a common story: namely, that the creator God had made a covenant with a chosen people (the Jews) and that they were to be the conduit by which God would bless all nations. In contrast to Judaism, however, early Christians regarded Jesus as the promised Messiah and through him the blessings promised to the Jewish people would reach out across the entire world.

Another notable, closely related idea is the early Christian belief that Jesus fulfilled various promises and prophecies recorded by the writers of the Hebrew Bible. The sacrifices, the centrality of the temple, even many of the commandments in the Torah, they concluded, had been fulfilled by the redemptive work of Jesus. For many early Christians, the destruction of the temple in 70 A.D. was confirmation that a new age had dawned and that Jesus was the means by which all people could experience the blessings of God.

Language and Expression

A significant challenge to readers of *The New Testament and the People of God* is the technical nature and scholarly style of the book. While much of the writing is lively and engaging, the subject matter is often quite technical, especially in the early chapters and requires slow and careful reading. As one scholar has described it, "The reading is often slow going, but what Wright has to say is very clear and utterly captivating."[4] Another scholar observes that "It is written in a very leisurely and at times repetitive style ... with tiny print for the text and microscopic print for the block quotes, footnotes, and bibliography" and that "Wright could have said what he needed to in 75-80% the amount of space."[5]

Those who have not studied hermeneutical theory before may find the first five chapters somewhat daunting. Also, the sheer complexity of first-century Judaism makes for a very detailed, though interesting study. The work is ultimately written for a scholarly readership and those with a basic knowledge of the New Testament will certainly find the book more manageable than those with only a limited background in the subject matter. Despite the technical nature of the book, however, few works have explored the diversity of first-century Judaism so comprehensively. Those wishing for a primer on first-century religious thought will find this a helpful introduction. Those with a deeper knowledge of the New Testament will be challenged by Wright's conclusions regarding the various ways in which Judaism influenced the thought and practice of its writers.

NOTES

1 The Jewish temple was destroyed in 70 A.D. by the Romans, following several years of insurrections. The Roman general Titus was responsible for the temple's destruction, as well as the execution of thousands of Jews, during his assault on the city of Jerusalem. In 73 A.D. Titus and his troops successfully defeated the Jewish fortress of Masada, which effectively ended the Jewish rebellion.

2 During the first century the Jewish people were under the rule of the Roman Empire. Although they were given freedom to worship, they desperately longed for independence.

3 Wright, *The New Testament*, 469.

4 Gilbert Bartholomew, Review of *The New Testament and the People of God*, Homiletic 19:2 (1994), 21.

5 Craig Blomberg, Review of *The New Testament and the People of God*, Criswell Theological Review 7 (1993), 125.

MODULE 6
SECONDARY IDEAS

KEY POINTS

- Wright defends a system of textual interpretation known as "critical realism."

- Ancient cultures often expressed their worldviews and theological beliefs through stories.

- An overlooked aspect of *The New Testament and the People of God* is Wright's unique conclusions about the eschatological hopes of Jews living in the first century.

Other Ideas

The secondary themes of N. T. Wright's *The New Testament and the People of God* include the value of an interpretive approach known as "critical realism,"* the use of stories in ancient cultures, and the eschatology of first-century Jews. With regard to his method of interpreting ancient writings, Wright advocates a system first introduced by Ben Meyer* known as "critical realism."[1] According to Wright:

> "This is a way of describing the process of 'knowing' that acknowledges the reality of the thing known, as something other than the knower (hence, "realism'), while also fully acknowledging that the only access we have to this reality lies along the spiraling path of appropriate dialogue or conversation between the knower and the thing known (hence 'critical'). This path leads to critical reflection on the products of our enquiry into "reality," so that our assertions about 'reality' acknowledge their own provisionality.* Knowledge, in other words, although in

> ❝ I suggest that human writing is best conceived as the articulation of worldviews, or, better still, the telling of stories which bring worldviews into articulation. ❞
>
> Wright, *The New Testament and the People of God*, 65

principle concerning realities independent of the knower, is never itself independent of the knower."[2]

This method of interpretation, Wright argues, is helpful in that it is an objective and informed method of understanding the history and religious thought of a given culture. The Bible, he suggests, should not be understood as a collection of writings disconnected from the world. The authors of the New Testament shared common assumptions about world history and the role and destiny of the Jewish people. This particular method of interpretation, he argues, helps to increase understanding of the world in which ancient documents were written and ultimately their meaning.

Wright contrasts "critical realism" with other methods, which he believes to be extreme and misguided. On the one hand there are those who argue that what is perceived by the senses cannot be trusted. On the other hand there are others, he believes, who are much too optimistic in their conclusion that what is perceived with our senses is an accurate representation of reality. Wright's "critical realism" represents an approach between these two extremes. His defense of the theory of "critical realism" is important for readers who continue on to the remaining books of the series *Christian Origins and the Question of God* as it is the interpretive approach employed throughout.

Exploring the Ideas

Several additional ideas and proposals emerge throughout *The New Testament and the People of God* that relate to Wright's ideas about interpretation. One notable example is his discussion of the important role that story-telling played in forming and spreading worldviews. Wright devotes much of the first five chapters—nearly 150 pages—to an exploration of how we might go about the thorny task of understanding the religious thought of ancient cultures. He suggests that ancient cultures often expressed and derived their beliefs through the retelling of stories. Ancient Jews, for example, understood themselves to be in a privileged relationship with the creator God. They believed that their ancestor Abraham received many promises from God, most notably for a homeland, which would belong to his descendants. However, because of his people's disobedience and neglect of the Torah, they were in a state of exile. This exile, they believed, would one day come to a decisive end when God would deliver his people from their enemies and usher in a period of unparalleled peace and blessing. The early Christians also believed that they stood in a privileged position with the creator God. In contrast to many of the Jews of their day, however, they believed that those who would experience the blessings promised to Abraham were not Jews who observed the various commandments found in the Torah, but those who followed Jesus as Lord. In both Judaism and Christianity, therefore, an understanding of significant events in history shaped religious thought.

Wright contends that human life "can be seen as grounded in and constituted by the implicit or explicit stories which humans tell themselves and one another."[3] This conclusion is important given Wright's presumption that both Judaism and Christianity should be regarded as a way of understanding world history rather than a mere religious system of unrelated doctrines created independently from historical events. Both Jews and Christians of the first century, Wright reasons, were not simply advocating a mélange of esoteric teachings, but a particular way of understanding world events and history. Christians and Jews both believed that they were the beneficiaries of

God's promises and that it was exclusively through their people that the God of Abraham sought to redeem humanity. Perceiving Christianity as a retelling or expansion of the story found in the Hebrew Bible is especially important, Wright suggests, for a proper understanding of the thought and teaching of the New Testament authors and the distinctive qualities of early Christianity. When Christianity is not understood in this light, it can easily be separated from its Jewish heritage, leading to a misunderstanding of its central teachings. Wright's discussion of this topic is illuminating and offers rich and helpful insights for readers, both students and academics, who wish to arrive at a greater understanding of the religious thought of first-century Jews and Christians.

Overlooked

One particular aspect of Wright's *The New Testament and the People of God* that has often been overlooked is his discussion of the nature and background of Jewish eschatology and apocalyptic literature. As Wright contends, Jews during the first century did not anticipate a sudden and abrupt end of the world, but looked forward to a future age when God would restore his people and bring healing to the world. According to Wright, "The hope of Israel, and of most special-interest groups within Israel, was not for post mortem disembodied bliss, but for a national liberation that would fulfil the expectations aroused by the memory, and regular celebration, of the exodus and, nearer at hand, of the Maccabean* victory. Hope focused on the coming of the kingdom of Israel's god."[4] This "coming of the kingdom," many Jews believed, would be accomplished through a decisive military victory in which a messianic figure would lead Israel in triumph over her enemies and usher in an age of peace and blessing.[5]

Early Christians, who came primarily from Jewish backgrounds, naturally shared many of these eschatological perspectives. Like their

Jewish counterparts, they longed for a coming age in which God would restore the world and bring about an earthly kingdom. For the Christians, this age had already been inaugurated by Jesus, though they were still waiting for its ultimate consummation and fulfilment. Jews and Christians disagreed as to how this kingdom would be established, but their understanding of its basic characteristics and the coming age were quite similar. In contrast to both Jews and Christians of the first century, many modern-day Christians have adopted an "other worldly" understanding of the coming age, contending that the present world will one day be destroyed and that individuals will experience the afterlife in some type of spirit realm. Wright's attention to the eschatological assumptions held by first-century Jews convincingly demonstrates that such an idea would not have been commonly held by first-century Jews nor, by implication, early Christians.

In recent years, the subject of the apocalyptic nature of Paul's letters has been addressed at length by Douglas Campbell* in his *The Deliverance of God: An Apocalyptic Rereading of Paul.*[6] Campbell relates the relevance of Paul's apocalyptic outlook to the current debate regarding the doctrine of justification and concludes that biblical scholars have for many centuries misunderstood Paul's teachings. He is critical of what he describes as "justification theory" and seeks to show how Paul's understanding of justification can be properly understood in the light of the apocalyptic nature of his letters.[7] Campbell's book has led to more scholarly attention on the subject of first-century apocalyptic literature and illustrates the complexity of Paul's understanding of justification. As scholars continue to grapple with the work of Wright and Campbell, popular Jewish perceptions of the coming eschatological age and the degree to which these persuasions were shared by early Christians will continue to be debated and explored. Scholars wishing to embark upon this task will undoubtedly find Wright's book to be a good foundation.

NOTES

1 See, especially, Ben Meyer, *Critical Realism and the New Testament*. Princeton Theological Monograph Series, Vol. 17 (Alison Park, PA.: Pickwick Publications, 1989).

2 Wright, *New Testament*, 35.

3 *Wright, New Testament*, 38.

4 *Wright, New Testament*, 169–70.

5 For a further discussion of Wright's treatment of Jewish eschatology, see Scott Hafemann, review of *The New Testament and the People of God*, by N.T. Wright, *Evangelical Theological Society* 40, no. 2 (1997): 305–8.

6 Douglas Campbell, *The Deliverance of God: An Apocalyptic Rereading of Paul* (Grand Rapids, Mich.: Eerdmans, 2009).

7 Campbell is critical of the way in which he believes modern Christianity has understood the nature of the Gospel. He is concerned that the Gospel is often understood in a way that is too individualistic, contractual, and conditional. In other words, he is critical of what he believes is an overemphasis on the traditional viewpoint, that salvation is offered on the condition that an individual accepts Jesus by faith, and believes that this understanding is built largely on a misreading of Romans 1–4. Campbell argues that Paul's understanding of salvation should be understood more as a divine initiative with certain results rather than as something that is dependent on man's response.

MODULE 7
ACHIEVEMENT

KEY POINTS

- Wright's work has successfully drawn attention to the importance of recognizing the Jewish background of the New Testament.

- The book's popularity may be attributed to Wright's substantive treatment in matters of scholarly interest.

- For readers with only a limited background in the literature of Second Temple Judaism, the book may be a challenge to comprehend.

Assessing the Argument

N.T.Wright's *The New Testament and the People of God* explores how a knowledge of the beliefs of Jews living in the first century enables modern readers to better understand several of the key subjects addressed in the New Testament .Wright argues that a proper understanding of the New Testament writers rests on the common Jewish assumptions of the time. These related to the place of Israel in world history, the role of the coming Jewish messiah, and the ways in which Jews understood the nature of the Mosaic Law. As Wright observes, "The reconstruction of the history of early Christianity must attempt to make sense of certain data within a coherent framework. It must put together the historical jigsaw of Judaism within its Greco-Roman world."[1] This focus on the importance of understanding the social, religious and political persuasions of the Jews of the first century has attracted a significant amount of scholarly attention. In *The New Testament and the People of God*

> ❝ The strengths of Wright's work are legion, not least the sheer volume of issues treated and the secondary literature mastered and cited. He thinks creatively, is willing to apply new approaches to well-worn subjects, [and] is not afraid to challenge liberal, scholarly consensus or popular evangelical piety. ❞
> Craig Blomberg, *Criswell Theological Review* 7 (1993), 125.

Wright reveals the religious world of the first century and so gives scholars a key to the worldview of the writers of the New Testament.

In addition to the strong case he makes for his thesis that the writers of the New Testament were heavily influenced by their Jewish background, Wright presents evidence for his controversial conclusion that Jews during the time of Jesus did not believe that the physical world would one day be destroyed. Rather than a future cataclysmic event that marks the end of the present age, Wright argues that Jews during the first century looked for God to restore and renew the earth, a belief which the early Christians believed was accomplished through the work of Jesus.

Achievement in Context

While few of Wright's key ideas are entirely original or altogether unique, his work has nonetheless received widespread acclaim for its treatment of first-century Judaism and how its beliefs may have influenced early Christians. The work itself does not seem to have been the result of a particular world event or of any cultural or political developments, though it is a thorough treatment of a topic that has received increasing attention in the scholarly community over the last few decades. Wright originally intended the book simply as an introduction to the remaining volumes in the *Christian Origins and the Question of God* series. However, as a result of the increased scholarly attention to the theology of Paul that took place after its publication, *The New Testament and the People of God* was soon regarded as a foundational work for those interested in a deeper examination of Christian origins and the beliefs of the early Christians.

The basic conclusions advocated by Wright have been adopted by several notable contemporary scholars, and, along with the writings of E.P. Sanders and James Dunn, have come to form the basis of the scholarly theory known as Covenantal Nomism.* Despite their differences on a number of matters, the movement as a whole has been quite influential and received considerable attention. This attention has been partly responsible for the popularity of many of Wright's subsequent works.

Limitations

The focus of Wright's book is his interpretation of ancient sources from the Second Temple period. As a result, it is difficult for those with only a limited knowledge of these primary sources to grasp his theories. While it may be used as an introduction to ancient Jewish literature, those wishing to interact with him on a more critical level must first become familiar with the relevant primary sources.

Readers of the book will do well to note the great diversity that characterized religious thought in the first century. Wright certainly acknowledges this diversity,[2] but many of his critics have suggested that he sometimes overlooks references in the primary sources in order to emphasize only particular aspects of first-century Jewish life.[3] Again, Wright portrays Christianity as a continuation of Judaism. However, many scholars and Christian leaders throughout church history have insisted that the Christian faith is quite different from Judaism and that the early followers of Jesus recognized this disparity. Wright has suggested that, while Christianity eventually came to stand on its own as a separate faith, many of the initial followers of Jesus were Jewish and saw no conflict between their Jewish faith and their worship of Jesus.

For these Jewish believers, Jesus was the Messiah of whom the Hebrew prophets spoke. Wright's discussion of these topics is compelling and convincing, but the reader should understand that these issues are still the subject of considerable scholarly debate.

NOTES

1   Wright, *New Testament*, 345.

2   See, for example, Wright, *New Testament*, 244. Here Wright acknowledges that "the one thing we can safely say about first-century Judaism is that there is no such thing as first-century Judaism, that it is best to speak of 'Judaisms,' plural."

3   See, for example, Johnson, book review, 537.

MODULE 8
PLACE IN THE AUTHOR'S WORK

KEY POINTS

- *The New Testament and the People of God* is the first volume of the series entitled *Christian Origins and the Question of God*.

- The primary historical observations made in this book are consistently upheld throughout Wright's later publications.

- *The New Testament and the People of God* was a seminal work that laid the foundation for several later volumes.

Positioning

N. T. Wright's *The New Testament and the People of God* is the first of six volumes in the series *Christian Origins and the Question of God*, published by SPCK and Fortress Press. Wright certainly builds on the subjects explored in this book in his subsequent volumes, but this book is clearly the work of a seasoned and accomplished scholar. This first book may be read on its own and it is useful to read it before the subsequent volumes in the series. In the first five chapters, Wright offers an extended prolegomena* in which he articulates his hermeneutical approach. He continues to use this same approach throughout the remainder of this book as well as the subsequent volumes of the series which at the present time include *Jesus and the Victory of God* (1997),[1] *The Resurrection of the Son of God* (2003),[2] and *Paul and the Faithfulness of God* (2013).[3] Wright plans to conclude the series with a volume on the Gospels and a final book devoted to early Christianity.

> **❝** The number of New Testament studies which are either literary or historical or theological are legion, and few have been the attempts at synthesis. N. T. Wright has sought to provide such a synthesis. **❞**
>
> Anthony Cross, *Journal for the Study of the New Testament* 53 (1994), 126.

Wright has published dozens of monographs and articles over the course of his career, but the series *Christian Origins and the Question of God* is widely regarded as his greatest literary achievement. At first glance, the volumes in the series may appear unrelated to one another, but Wright demonstrates that this is not the case. As he reflects in the preface to *The New Testament and the People of God*, the subjects of Paul and Jesus "belonged together more closely than I had realized. Both were concerned with the historical description of events and beliefs in the first century. Both emphasized a particular way of understanding the relevant texts and events. Both required a pre-understanding of first-century Judaism. Both demanded concluding theological and practical reflections."[4]

Integration

Throughout the series *Christian Origins and the Question of God*, Wright demonstrates how a well-informed understanding of first-century Judaism is essential for interpreting the New Testament and explaining the rise of Christianity. The subsequent volumes in the series follow the same methodology as the first, and Wright remains consistent in his conclusions throughout.

Some of the primary themes found in *The New Testament and the People of God* were addressed in a book Wright published only one year earlier, *The Climax of the Covenant: Christ and the Law in Pauline Theology*.[5] In this scholarly work, Wright demonstrated how the death and resurrection of Christ fundamentally influenced the ways in which early Christian writers such as the Apostle Paul understood the nature of the Church, the Mosaic Law, and the relationship between the two. Wright concluded that the death and resurrection of Christ fulfilled the Mosaic Law and ushered in a new age in which Gentiles were to be welcomed into the covenant community. They would not, though, be obliged to observe the various commandments of the Mosaic Law, which marked the identity of the Jewish people (*e.g.*, circumcision,* Sabbath* observance, dietary restrictions, observance of Jewish festivals* and so on).

In addition to the *Christian Origins and the Question of God* series and the earlier work *The Climax of the Covenant*, *The New Testament and the People of God* laid the groundwork for several future publications relating to the Gospels, the Apostle Paul, and a variety of other theological subjects. A common feature of all of Wright's scholarly works is the extensive examination of the primary documents of the early church and of Jews living during the Second Temple period. He first established this practice of investigating historical documents to ascertain the theological convictions of the New Testament authors with the volume *The New Testament and the People of God*.

Significance

Given Wright's long and illustrious writing career, it is unlikely that he will be most remembered for his work *The New Testament and the People of God*. Nevertheless, it was the book which first led to his status of a premier New Testament scholar and theologian. As one writer has observed, "One might easily take Tom Wright's *The New Testament and the People of God* as just another text on 'New Testament Background.' That would be a grave mistake; [Wright's] book is a *tour de force* of synthetic historical imagination. It is a book which immediately locates Wright among the most important NT scholars of our time."[6]

The book has been generally warmly received in the academic community and its impact has been significant. While there are many who have criticized some of Wright's conclusions, there has been considerable praise for his work on those primary sources that relate to first-century Judaism and the early church. Of course, not everyone has been willing to embrace his interpretation of first-century Judaism or the teachings of Paul.[7] However, while there is no consensus on the validity of his arguments as yet, Wright has been persuasive in emphasizing the benefits of properly understanding the common theological beliefs of first-century Jews. Scholarly debate regarding the nature of first-century Judaism and its influence on New Testament authors will undoubtedly continue for many decades. As scholars continue to discuss these issues, *The New Testament and the People of God* will surely remain at the center of this dialogue.

NOTES

1   Wright, *Jesus and the Victory of God*.

2   Wright, *The Resurrection of the Son of God*.

3   Wright, *Paul and the Faithfulness of God*.

4   Wright, *New Testament and the People of God*, XIII.

5   Wright, *The Climax of the Covenant*.

6   Adam, Book Review, 164.

7   Works critical of Wright include John Piper, *The Future of Justification: A Response to N.T. Wright* (Nottingham: Inter-Varsity Press, 2008); Gathercole, *Where is Boasting?*; and Mark Seifrid, *Christ, Our Righteousness: Paul's Theology of Justification* (Downers Grove, Il.: IVP Academic, 2001).

SECTION 3
IMPACT

MODULE 9
THE FIRST RESPONSES

KEY POINTS

- Biblical scholars have occasionally criticized Wright's portrayal of Second Temple Judaism.

- Wright has argued that he recognizes the divergence within Second Temple Judaism and also contends that his critics have often misunderstood him.

- Given the theological implications of his work, Wright's *The New Testament and the People of God* remains at the forefront of scholarly discussion.

Criticism

Given the breadth of N.T.Wright's *The New Testament and the People of God* and its profound theological implications, it should come as little surprise that some scholars have objected to his portrayals of first-century Judaism, early Christianity, or to some of Wright's conclusions. Luke Timothy Johnson,* for example, argues that "Wright gives only five pages to the entire Greco-Roman context (pages 152–57), and even less to the Diaspora.*"[1]

Though Wright readily acknowledges the complexities of first-century Judaism, he has been criticized by Johnson and others for drawing what they consider to be rigid conclusions that do not allow for the many diverse viewpoints held by Jews during the first century.[2] Wright, however, has remained quite consistent in his conclusion that Jews of the time shared a common worldview that included at the very least the conviction that they were God's chosen people and beneficiaries of the covenant God had made with their forefather Abraham.*[3]

> ❝ Since I am aware of the virtual certainty of error in some of what I write, I hope I shall pay proper attention to the comments of those—and no doubt there will be many—who wish to draw my attention to the places where they find my statement of the evidence inadequate, my arguments weak, or my conclusions unwarranted. ❞
>
> Wright, *The New Testament and the People of God*, XVII-XVIII

In more recent years, several of the theological viewpoints espoused by Wright were the focus of a significant rebuttal by John Piper,* a well-known American evangelical pastor and scholar. Piper's criticisms are related primarily to Wright's exegesis* of various New Testament texts. He argues that Wright's conclusions about Paul in particular, while innovative, distort Paul's teaching about the Gospel. As he states:

"It may be that in his own mind and heart Wright has a clear and firm grasp on the gospel of Christ and the biblical meaning of justification. But in my judgment, what he has written will lead to a kind of preaching that will not announce clearly what makes the lordship of Christ good news for guilty sinners or show those who are overwhelmed with sin how they may stand righteous in the presence of God."[4]

Piper's concerns are clearly theological and pastoral. Interestingly, the works of Wright seem to have been received somewhat more warmly by academics than by ministers.

Responses

In the years following the release of *The New Testament and the People of God*, Wright actively engaged with a number of biblical scholars who objected to various aspects of his work. Perhaps most notably, in 2009 he published the succinctly titled work *Justification: God's Plan and Paul's Vision*.[5] This book was written primarily in response to John Piper's criticism of his understanding of the doctrine of justification. Traditionally, it has been understood that when the Apostle Paul spoke of justification he was referring to the event of salvation whereby God redeems the individual and sets him or her apart as a member of the family of God. Wright, on the other hand, has argued that justification refers not to the event of salvation, but merely to the judicial pronouncement in which God declares that a person is already part of the covenant community. In other words, Wright argues that justification is an event that occurs after an individual enters into a covenantal relationship with God, not the act which serves as the basis of individual salvation.

Wright's response to Piper was rather blunt: "the problem is that he [Piper] hasn't listened to what I'm saying."[6] Wright insists that readers of Paul have for many years been influenced by the legacy of the Reformation and so read the Bible as though it were written in the sixteenth century and shared the same concerns as Martin Luther. When Paul condemns the "works of the Law," Wright reasons, he was not condemning a system of "works righteousness" as Luther believed, but was concerned specifically with the observance of such markers of Jewish identity as Sabbath keeping, circumcision, kosher*, the observation of Jewish festivals, etc. Wright believes that these practices were not to be demanded of Gentile Christians in large part because they were only intended to be temporary and because they were fracturing the Christian community.

Conflict and Consensus

Given that a consensus has yet to form with respect to the nature of first-century Judaism and the events that brought about the rise of Christianity, Wright's *The New Testament and the People of God* remains an important achievement of continued scholarly interest. While his treatment of primary Jewish sources is not exhaustive, he does discuss a number of important extant sources at length in his effort to reveal the religious, political, and social environment in which the New Testament was written.

Wright's historical work is not an end in itself, of course; it has far-reaching implications for how the Christian Gospel is to be understood. When engaging in historical study, Wright also maintains an eye for the theological significance of his findings. His challenges to traditional assumptions about early Christianity and the teachings of the Apostle Paul have created significant interest.

Scholars have remained fairly consistent in both their praise and criticism of Wright's book. Although the nature of the debate has changed slightly in the last few decades, the views of the proponents and opponents of the New Perspective of Paul have changed very little. This is not to say that the conversation about first-century Judaism or Paul's understanding of justification is stagnant or that interest in the subject has waned. A number of scholarly journals and monographs continue to be published each year that explore one or more aspects of first-century Judaism or early Christianity. The Jewish literature from the time of Paul is, in fact, quite substantial and a considerable amount of evidence remains for scholars to consider. Wright's conclusions are likely to be continually re-examined in the light of these fresh studies.

NOTES

1   Luke Timothy Johnson, review of *The New Testament and the People of God*, by Nicholas Thomas Wright, *Journal of Biblical Literature* 113, no. 3 (1994): 537.

2   Those critical of Wright include Piper, *The Future of Justification:* Gathercole, *Where is Boasting*; and Mark Seifrid, *Christ, Our Righteousness*. While Piper is critical of Wright mainly on theological grounds, Gathercole offers criticisms that of Wright's work that are more historical in nature.

3   See Genesis 15:1–16.

4   Piper, *The Future of Justification*, 15.

5   Wright, *Justification*.

6   Wright, *Justification*, 5.

THE EVOLVING DEBATE

KEY POINTS

- Wright provides fresh insights relating to the common beliefs of first-century Jews and the degree to which these beliefs were shared by early Christians.

- His scholarly works are part of the foundations of the schools of thought known as Covenantal Nomism and the New Perspective of Paul.

- Though they are not always in agreement, E. P. Sanders and James Dunn have defended many of Wright's views.

Uses and Problems

Wright's *The New Testament and the People of God* has been largely successful in its aim to emphasize the importance of first-century Judaism in the context of the New Testament. His emphasis on the importance of primary documents from early Christianity and Second Temple Judaism has ignited a renewed scholarly interest in them. Much contemporary biblical scholarship is now concerned with what these texts may reveal about the religious assumptions held by the authors of the New Testament, including the Apostle Paul.

Wright's study of first-century Judaism has served as the basis for many of his subsequent later publications, in which he has examined the theology of Paul and the beliefs of the early church.[1] Wright has s contended, for example, that Paul's doctrine of justification and the related doctrine of imputation* have often been fundamentally misunderstood, especially since the time of the Protestant Reformation.

> ❝ It is vital to stress, not least for anyone coming fresh to all these discussions, that there has never been one single coherent thing that can be called the 'new perspective.' People often write as if Ed Sanders, James Dunn and I formed a united front. But we ... have always had serious and significant differences from one another. ❞
>
> N. T. Wright, *Justification*

Although there remains much debate about the precise nature of first-century Judaism, Wright's work—both *The New Testament and the People of God* as well as many of his subsequent volumes—has brought about a rise of scholarly interest in the religious worldview of first-century Jews as well as challenges to Wright's own conclusions.[2] Prior to its publication, only a few scholars had explored the world of first-century Judaism and its relevance to the New Testament.[3] For the most part, these works were either overlooked or studied only by a small number of specialists.

Schools of Thought

Based in part on the publications of N. T. Wright, including *The New Testament and the People of God,* two influential schools of thought have developed. The first movement is referred to as "Covenantal Nomism." This is essentially the belief that Jews living in the first century were not attempting to earn individual salvation by strictly observing the numerous laws found in the Mosaic Law. Based on their reading of Jewish literature from the Second Temple period, proponents of this school of thought have concluded that the motivation to follow the Law of Moses was not to receive salvation, but to retain their identity as a distinct people, and, perhaps more importantly, to maintain their status as God's covenantal people. The basis of their salvation, therefore, was not individual acts of piety or obedience to various laws, but their covenantal status.

More recently, the debate about the nature of first-century Judaism has turned to questions that concern the theology of the Apostle Paul. In particular, Wright has argued that over the last several centuries there has been a common misreading of Paul's understanding of the doctrine of justification. This is based on the mistaken notion that Jews during the first century were attempting to earn salvation by fidelity to the Mosaic Law.[4] Based on the manner in which Covenantal Nomism understands the nature of first-century Judaism, Wright has argued extensively that when Paul expressed criticism of those observing certain laws in the Torah, he was not condemning a system of "works righteousness." Instead, he was concerned that the continued observance of such laws as circumcision, dietary regulations, Sabbath keeping and so on were counter-productive because they needlessly divided believing Gentiles from believing Jews.

In Current Scholarship

In addition to Wright, two other notable scholars have defended the movements known as Covenental Nomism and the New Perspective on Paul. In 1977, E. P. Sanders published *Paul and Palestinian Judaism*.[5] This book sparked a fresh examination of Paul's understanding of the Jewish Law and the doctrine of justification. Sanders proposed that much of the traditional teaching on Paul was fundamentally misguided and in need of revision. Key for Sanders was his conclusion that first-century Judaism was not the legalistic "works-righteousness" religious system that many had assumed. Instead, he reasoned, Jews during the first century saw themselves as part of an elect community and their preservation in this community required their continued obedience to the Mosaic Law. Sanders, in basic agreement with Wright, has argued that this obedience was not the basis of membership in the covenant community, but rather a way to demonstrate your membership.

Many of the ideas championed by Wright have also been advocated by New Testament scholar James Dunn, who for many years was the Lightfoot Professor of Divinity at the University of Durham. Dunn's major book on the subject is *The New Perspective on Paul.*[6] Like Sanders, Dunn argues against the general viewpoint that first-century Judaism might be described as a "work-righteousness" type of faith in which salvation was achieved on the basis of observing the Law. Wright, Dunn, Sanders and other advocates of the movement are not in complete agreement about the precise nature of Paul's theology. They do, though, all agree that Christians, especially those living in the post-Enlightenment period,* have severely misread Paul due to a false portrayal of first-century Judaism.

NOTES

1   In addition to *The New Testament and the People of God*, Wright has written a number of books which discuss the nature of first-century Judaism and/ or Paul's understanding of justification and other related themes. These works include *The Climax of the Covenant*; *Jesus and the Victory of God*; *Justification*; *Paul and the Faithfulness of God*; *Paul: Fresh Perspectives*; and *What St Paul Really Said.*

2   In addition to a number of scholarly articles and biblical commentaries, several monographs have discussed the merits of the New Perspective on Paul and Covenantal Nomism, such as Douglas Campbell, *The Deliverance of God*; Robert Cara, *Cracking the Foundation of the New Perspective on Paul* (Fearn, U.K.; Christian Focus Publications, 2017); James Dunn, *The New Perspective on Paul* (Grand Rapids, Mich.: Eerdmans, 2007); Gathercole, *Where is Boasting?*; Colin Kruse, *Paul, the Law, and Justification* (Eugene, Oreg.: Wipf & Stock, 2008); Piper, *The Future of Justification*; Seifrid, *Christ, Our Righteousness;* Peter Stuhlmacher, *Revisiting Paul's Doctrine of Justification: A Challenge to the New Perspective* (Downers Grove, Il.: IVP Academic, 2001); Chris VanLandingham, *Judgment and Justification in Early Judaism and the Apostle Paul* (Grand Rapids, Mich.: Baker Academic, 2006); Guy Waters, *Justification and the New Perspectives on Paul: A Review and Response* (Phillipsburg, NJ: P&R Publishing, 2004); and Stephen Westerholm, *Justification Reconsidered: Rethinking a Pauline Theme* (Grand Rapids, Mich.: Eerdmans, 2013).

3   Early studies laying the foundation for the New Perspective on Paul and the theory known as Covenantal Nomism include Stendahl's, "The Apostle Paul and the Introspective Conscience of the West," and Sanders's, *Paul and Palestinian Judaism*.

4   See, for example, *The Climax of the Covenant*; *Justification*; *Paul and the Faithfulness of God*; *Paul: Fresh Perspectives*; and *What St Paul Really Said*.

5   Sanders, *Paul and Palestinian Judaism.*

6   Dunn, *The New Perspective on Paul.*

MODULE 11
IMPACT AND INFLUENCE TODAY

KEY POINTS

* *The New Testament and the People of God* remains an important scholarly work.

* Scholars influenced by the writings of Martin Luther have been especially resistant to Wright's ideas.

* Criticism of Wright's book has often been related to theological matters though historians have also disagreed with some of his conclusions.

Position

Its scholarly treatment of first-century Judaism and early Christianity has kept N.T.Wright's *The New Testament and the People of God* relevant to the contemporary debate. Since its publication there has been a renewed interest in the New Testament's historical setting and the core beliefs of its authors. Many scholars have researched the relevant primary sources in order to reach a more definitive understanding of the many Jewish movements of the first century as well as the common religious and political assumptions and aspirations held by Jews at the time. These subjects are vast, of course, and the debate continues about various aspects of Judaism at the time the New Testament was written. As the debates and research continue into the fundamental beliefs of first-century Jews and early Christians, the works of Wright will remain at the heart of the discussion.

The implications of Wright's conclusions are far reaching and can face opposition. Scholars holding to a soteriology* similar to that of Martin Luther have found his proposals particularly challenging and problematic. Some have found Wright's work persuasive though not

> ❝ One of the greatest difficulties in present-day biblical scholarship is the explosion of aims, methods and approaches, so that true debate becomes difficult, there being fewer fixed points from which to begin. It is important to be clear about one's own starting points, and that is what those earlier treatments were meant to offer. ❞
>
> Wright, *Paul and the Faithfulness of God*, xvii

all have been convinced by his evidence. The implications of his scholarly work are such, however, that it continues to demand consideration.

Interaction

Several of the more notable conclusions made by Wright in *The New Testament and the People of God* have indirectly challenged more conservative scholars, particularly those who, hold a view of the Christian doctrine of salvation that Wright believes to be at odds with his historical studies of first-century Judaism and early Christianity. Many conservative scholars have, in fact, found Wright's conclusions to be plausible, but some have expressed reservations that his views are out of step with the traditional understanding of the doctrine of justification. One of the more vocal opponents to Wright has been the American pastor and scholar John Piper who published a critique of Wright's theological viewpoints in 2008.[1]

Scholars with a Lutheran* background in Germany and elsewhere have not found many of Wright's conclusions easy to accept. Central to Martin Luther's interpretation of the New Testament was his belief that the Jews of the first century were steeped in what may be described as a "works-righteousness" type of religion; that is, the belief that one can obtain salvation on the basis of performing good works and keeping the various commandments of the Mosaic Law. Wright challenges this view, arguing that first-century Judaism was not predominantly occupied with performing good deeds in order to gain salvation. Rather, the Jews of the time sought to maintain the observance of the Law as part of their already established covenantal relationship with God. Given that Wright's teaching runs counter to the teachings of Martin Luther, it is not surprising that his conclusions about Judaism in the first century or his interpretation of Paul's writings have not been received with eagerness in Lutheran settings.

The Continuing Debate

Several well-known biblical scholars have defended what they consider to be the traditional understanding of the doctrine of justification against the claims of Wright. John Piper, Simon Gathercole, * Mark Seifrid, * Chris VanLandingham, * Colin Kruse, * Peter Stuhlmacher, * Guy Waters, * Robert Cara, * and others have responded to Wright's interpretation of the New Testament as well as his understanding of first-century Judaism.[2] These scholars have objected to various aspects of Wright's reading of ancient texts, while others have concluded that, after further review of the relevant primary sources, his understanding of first-century Judaism cannot be defended in all cases. Some of the objections raised have derived from pastoral concerns, while other critics have reached their conclusions on a purely scholarly level.

Both proponents and opponents of Wright's scholarship recognize the significant theological implications of his work. At the center of the debate is the nature of the Christian doctrine of justification. This doctrine addresses how each individual relates to God and the means by which one may be made right in the sight of God. For those involved in the debate, therefore, Wright's work is not merely academic in nature but has profound theological implications. Wright's opponents fear that he has misrepresented the Christian Gospel and his work will result in either widespread confusion or a distortion of New Testament teachings. His supporters, however, argue that the traditional understanding of Christian doctrines such as justification are in need of greater clarity or even correction.

NOTES

1   Piper, *The Future of Justification*.

2   *Ibid*.; Gathercole, *Where is Boasting?*; Seifrid, *Christ, Our Righteousness*; VanLandingham, *Judgment and Justification in Early Judaism and the Apostle Paul*; Kruse, *Paul, the Law, and Justification*; Stuhlmacher, *Revisiting Paul's Doctrine of Justification*; Waters, *Justification and the New Perspectives on Paul*; Cara, *Cracking the Foundation of the New Perspective on Paul*.

MODULE 12
WHERE NEXT?

KEY POINTS

- Wright's *The New Testament and the People of God* will continue to serve as a notable text and the scholarly foundation for many of his subsequent books.

- Other scholars have supported many of the ideas presented by Wright in *The New Testament and the People of God*, though with modifications.

- Wright's *The New Testament and the People of God* is a groundbreaking work and provides significant insights into the beliefs of early Christians.

Potential

N. T. Wright's *The New Testament and the People of God* promises to remain a relevant text in the academic disciplines of theology and New Testament studies. Scholarly interest in the world of first-century Judaism has only increased in recent decades while those involved with the theology of the Apostle Paul will undoubtedly continue to engage with Wright's work.

The book is likely to retain significant influence, though this may be limited to the scholarly community. *The New Testament and the People of God* is the first of six volumes in the series *Christian Origins and the Question of God*. While it is certainly valuable in its own right, much of its continued influence will come from its role in preparing the reader for the remaining books in the series, particularly the fourth entitled *Paul and the Faithfulness of God*. It is in this fourth book that Wright has most exhaustively incorporated his earlier research from *The New Testament and the People of God* into his study of the theology

> **❝** Something must now be said about the scope of this first volume. It is basically an exercise in ground-clearing, designed to enable me to engage in further work on Jesus, Paul and the Gospels.... In most of this book, then, I write as a fascinated amateur, rather than a highly-trained professional. **❞**
>
> Wright, *The New Testament and the People of God*, xvi

of the Apostle Paul. In reference to this volume, Wright remarks that "all kinds of things I might have said by way of preliminaries are to be found in the earlier volumes, particularly *NTPG*."[1]

All the indications are that scholars will continue to analyze and develop a number of Wright's proposals in the coming years. The complexities of first-century Judaism, for example, are notorious. In addition to a vast number of ancient primary sources, the study is further complicated by the disagreements among the Jewish people themselves on theological and political matters. In spite of these complexities, the importance of the subject will no doubt give rise to further analysis and scholarly attention, much of which will undoubtedly be centered upon the *The New Testament and the People of God*.

Future Directions

Given the depth and complexities of this book and its relatively recent publication, it is difficult to speculate which scholars will continue to defend the theses presented by Wright in *The New Testament and the People of God*. Its subject matter generally evokes very nuanced positions in which some conclusions are accepted while others are rejected.

One example of this is the recent work of John Barclay* entitled *Paul and the Gift*.[2] Barclay agrees with that first-century Judaism appreciated and affirmed the concept of grace with regard to salvation and that it was not a religion in which salvation had to be earned by obedience to the Law of Moses. He has also advocated, along with Wright, that the early Christians, most notably Paul, were intent on proclaiming the Christian Gospel to all of mankind given their belief that salvation was available to all, whether Jew or Greek. However, Barclay has emphasized some matters that he believes were overlooked by Wright. In particular, he has investigated the practice of gift giving in ancient cultures and how this relates to the concept of grace as expressed in the New Testament writings of Romans and Galatians.

Summary

The New Testament and the People of God is a fresh examination of the life and times of Jesus and the Apostles. In his examination of this complex period of world history, Wright makes substantial contributions to our understanding of first-century Judaism and the beliefs of early Christians. After several introductory chapters in which he discusses his methodology, Wright provides an extensive overview of Jewish beliefs in the first century.

On the basis of his extensive survey of primary sources, Wright argues that early Christianity was inescapably Jewish in many important aspects of its theology. The implications of this conclusion are great, not least in how Wright understands the theology of the Gospel writers and the Apostle Paul. These findings have served as the basis for extended conversation amongst biblical scholars.

While many of the ideas expressed in the book cannot rightly be regarded as original, it remains very influential, in large part because it is one of the most ambitious and scholarly attempts to articulate those ideas. Wright is one of several notable scholars who have advanced what has come to be known as the New Perspective on Paul. Building upon the pioneering work of E. P. Sanders,[3] *The New*

Testament and the People of God has come to be regarded as a foundational text for those interested in the beliefs of the early Christians and their relationship to the beliefs of ancient Judaism.

NOTES

1   Wright, *Paul and the Faithfulness of God*, xvii.

2   John Barclay, *Paul and the Gift* (Grand Rapids, Mich.: Eerdmans, 2015).

3   Sanders, *Paul and Palestinian Judaism*.

GLOSSARY

GLOSSARY OF TERMS

Anglican Church: a Christian religious body comprised mainly of churches belonging to the Church of England.

Covenant (adjective: "covenantal"): a solemn agreement or pledge agreed upon by two parties. Many covenants ratified in the ancient world and in the Bible were between a greater and a lesser party (e.g., God and Abraham) and entailed a promise of faithfulness, obedience, and loyalty from the lesser party and some type of benefit or reward to be granted by the greater party.

Covenantal Nomism: a scholarly theory that Jews living in the first century were not attempting to earn salvation from God by strictly observing the numerous laws found in the Old Testament.

Circumcision: a medical procedure, practiced on all Jewish males, which is usually performed eight days after birth. It was first practiced by Abraham and has served as one of the more notable identity-markers of the Jewish people ever since.

Critical Realism: a philosophical system of thought that affirms that one can obtain knowledge of something independent of oneself but that this knowledge is not subjectively obtained.

Diaspora: the relocation during several periods of Jewish history of Jews to locations outside of Palestine. Many Jews in the first century fled their homeland as a result of persecution and settled in various locations throughout the Greco-Roman world.

Eschatology (adjective: "eschatological"): the study of the last things, that is, the events that precipitate and accompany the end of the world or the current age. "Apocalyptic" literature is typically characterized by dramatic and sometimes allegorical descriptions of the events that will occur in the final days.

Essenes: a religious sect in first-century Judaism known for their ascetic lifestyle. Many believe that the famous Dead Sea Scrolls, which were discovered in 1947, were produced in an Essene community.

Exegesis: the actual process of interpreting and drawing out the meaning of a literary text.

Gentiles: a general word used in reference to non-Jews. In some contexts, the term may be also be used to describe the people groups or nations outside Israel.

Gospels: the four principle writings in the New Testament, which provide an account of the life and ministry of Jesus. While there were many gospels written in early Christianity, it was the Gospels of Matthew, Mark, Luke and John that the early church regarded as authoritative.

Hebrew Bible: the primary literary works of the Jewish faith that were written in the Hebrew language before the first century. When translated they are typically referred to collectively as "The Old Testament" by those in the Christian tradition.

Hermeneutics: principles applying to the art and science of interpreting a literary text.

Imputation: traditionally understood as the means by which Christians receive the righteousness of God. There is debate as to whether imputation is actual or only forensic, that is, merely a declaration.

Jewish Festivals: major events in the Jewish calendar. Some of the more notable include Passover, the Feast of Unleavened Bread, First fruits, Pentecost (or Feast of Weeks), the Day of Atonement, and the Feast of Tabernacles. According to Exodus 23:14–19, all Jewish males were required to travel to Jerusalem for the feasts of Unleavened Bread, Pentecost, and Tabernacles.

Justification: theological term referring to the act of acquitting or declaring an individual to be free of guilt. The Apostle Paul frequently addressed the subject of justification, that is, how one might be found innocent before God.

Kosher: specific foods that have been approved for consumption by Jewish rabbinic authorities. The biblical books of Leviticus and Deuteronomy make a distinction between foods that are "clean" and foods that are "unclean." Foods that are kosher have been determined to be clean.

Lutheranism: a Protestant tradition inspired by the sixteenth-century theologian, Martin Luther.

New Perspective on Paul: a scholarly theory that the Apostle Paul articulated his doctrine of justification by faith not as a correction to the belief that one can earn salvation by obedience to the laws of Moses, but as a correction to the belief that one can earn salvation by being Jewish.

New Testament: the 27 volumes traditionally believed to have been written during the first century which Christians have regarded as authoritative for matters pertaining to theology and the Christian life.

Maccabean Period: the period in Jewish history during the second century B.C. in which the Jews rebelled against foreign powers such as the Seleucids under the leadership of Mattathias and his sons.

Messiah: the individual Jews and Christians believe will be sent by God in the final days. Christians have traditionally understood that Jesus fulfilled this role.

Mosaic Law: the ancient law of the Hebrews, traditionally ascribed to Moses and recorded in the Old Testament books of Exodus, Leviticus, Numbers, and Deuteronomy.

Pauline Epistles: writings traditionally ascribed to the Apostle Paul. Contemporary scholars have reached a consensus that Paul was the author of Romans, 1 Corinthians, 2 Corinthians, Galatians, Philippians, 1 Thessalonians, and Philemon. Debates persist regarding the authenticity of Ephesians, Colossians, 2 Thessalonians, 1 Timothy, 2 Timothy, and Titus.

Pharisees: the largest and most influential religious and political party during the first century. They were based in Jerusalem, and sought to uphold the laws prescribed by Moses.

Post-Enlightenment Period: a general reference to the period of time between the nineteenth century and the present.

Prolegomena: a discussion of preliminary matters the author believes are relevant to the material discussed in the remainder of the volume. The term should not be equated with the word "introduction" as the former is not simply an overview of a work but a preliminary discussion of topics the author believes to be relevant to his work.

Protestant Reformation: a series of events that eventually led to a split in Christianity between the Roman Catholic Church and the Protestant Church.

Provisionality: a state of being that is temporary and/or conditional in nature.

Roman Catholic Church: the largest Christian tradition which looks to the Bishop of Rome (the Pope) as its leader.

Roman Empire: the political kingdom of the Romans established in approximately the first century B.C.

Sabbath: recognized by Jews as the seventh day of the week (Saturday) and regarded as a day of rest. The practice is fashioned after the creation week recorded in Genesis 1–3.

Sadducees: an influential religious and political party during the first century. They are believed to have been much more moderate in their theological persuasions than the Pharisees. Several of the Sadducees are believed to have been members of the Jewish Sanhedrin, that is, the elite ruling body in first-century Judaism. Like the Pharisees, the Sadducees were hostile to the teaching of Jesus.

Second Temple Judaism: term often used to describe the period of time between the completion of the second Jewish temple in the sixth century BC and its destruction by the Romans in 70CE.

Soteriology: the study of the Christian doctrine of salvation.

Torah: refers to the first five books of the Hebrew Bible and is often translated as "law." In a more specific sense, it is used to describe the portion of the Hebrew Bible that contains the individual laws. This portion of Scripture is foundational to Judaism.

Westminster Abbey: an abbey/church located in London, England that was first constructed in the tenth century.

Works Righteousness: a religious system of thought in which salvation is understood to be earned on the basis of moral living or obedience to a set of commandments.

PEOPLE MENTIONED IN THE TEXT

Abraham, also known as Abram, is traditionally believed to have lived around the eighteenth century, B.C.E. He is known as the patriarch of Judaism and Islam.

A. K. M. Adam (b. 1957) is a biblical scholar currently serving as a tutor in New Testament and Greek at St. Stephen's House, Oxford. His scholarly research has focused on the science of biblical interpretation, the Gospel of Matthew, and the Epistle of James.

Augustine of Hippo (354–430 C.E.) was a Christian theologian from Hippo in Northern Africa. His biographical writings are known simply as the *Confessions*.

John Barclay (b. 1958) is a British New Testament scholar who currently serves as the Lightfoot Professor of Divinity at Durham University in England. His scholarly research has focused primarily on the writings of the Apostle Paul.

George Caird (1917–1984) was a British biblical scholar who taught for many years in North America and the United Kingdom. His scholarly research extended to a number of fields including the New Testament Gospels and the Pauline Epistles.

Douglas Campbell (b. 1961) currently serves as Professor of New Testament at Duke Divinity School. Campbell's scholarly publications mainly focus upon the historical background of the Apostle Paul's letters and various aspects of Paul's theology.

Robert Cara currently serves as the Hugh and Sallie Reaves Professor of New Testament at Reformed Theological Seminary in Charlotte, North Carolina. Cara's scholarly interests include Second Temple Judaism and the writings of the Apostle Paul.

James Dunn (b. 1939) is a retired British New Testament scholar who taught for many years at the University of Durham, in England. Along with Sanders and Wright, Dunn is one of the principle proponents of the New Perspective on Paul, a scholarly movement which has attempted to redefine first-century Judaism.

Thomas Stearns (T. S.) Eliot (1888–1965) was a British writer and literary critic who received the Nobel Peace prize for literature in 1948. Eliot is widely acclaimed for his poetic writings.

Simon Gathercole is a British New Testament scholar who currently serves as Lecturer in New Testament Studies at the University of Cambridge. He completed his doctoral studies under the supervision of James Dunn at the University of Durham, in England and has produced scholarly works on the Apostle Paul, the Gospels, and early Christian literature.

Jesus was a first-century Jew known primarily for his revolutionary teaching and miracles. Many of his followers believe that he was resurrected from the dead following his crucifixion in Jerusalem.

Luke Timothy Johnson (b. 1943) is an American New Testament scholar who presently serves as the Robert Woodruff Professor of New Testament and Christian Origins at Candler School of Theology in Atlanta, Georgia. Johnson has written extensively on early Christianity and various New Testament writings.

Josephus was an important first-century Jewish historian known for, among other things, his writings about the Jewish conflicts with Rome and the destruction of the Jerusalem temple in 70 A.D.

Colin Kruse is an Anglican New Testament scholar teaching at Melbourne School of Theology, in Australia. In addition to his scholarly research on the theology of Paul, he has published a number of biblical commentaries on various New Testament writings.

C. S. Lewis (1898–1963) was a British scholar and writer who taught for many years at the University of Oxford and the University of Cambridge. His works often pertained to Christian theology and included *The Screwtape Letters, Mere Christianity*, and *The Chronicles of Narnia*.

Martin Luther (1483–1546) was a German theologian and churchman who became one of the more notable reformers of the 16th century. He contended that the Roman Church was falsely teaching that an individual must perform many commandments and good deeds in order to experience salvation.

Ben Meyer (1927–1995) was a literary critic and writer who taught for several years at McMaster University in Canada. Meyer wrote extensively on the historical Jesus, early Christianity, and Christian hermeneutics.

The Apostle Paul was a first-century Jew known for travelling throughout the Greco-Roman world and establishing Christian communities. He is known primarily today as the author of many of the New Testament writings.

John Piper (b. 1946) is an American theologian and retired pastor. The ministry Desiring God is based upon his book of the same title.

E. P. Sanders (b. 1937) is an American New Testament scholar who, prior to his retirement, taught for several years at Duke University in North Carolina. Sanders is known primarily for his pioneering work on first-century Judaism.

Peter Stuhlmacher (b. 1932) is a former professor of New Testament at the University of Tübingen, Germany. He has written a number of scholarly books on Paul and the Gospels.

Mark Seifrid is a New Testament scholar currently teaching at Concordia Seminary in St. Louis, Missouri. Seifrid is known primarily for his scholarly publication on the theology of the Apostle Paul.

Krister Stendahl (1921–2008) was a Swedish New Testament scholar and clergyman in the Church of Sweden. Stendahl was known primarily for his scholarship of early Christianity and the theology of the Apostle Paul.

Chris VanLandingham is a New Testament scholar who has taught at Oral Roberts University and St Gregory's University. VanLandingham is known for this research on the Apostle Paul, specifically Paul's understanding of the doctrine of justification.

Guy Waters currently serves as the James Baird Professor of New Testament at the Reformed Theological Seminary in Jackson, Tennessee. His research has focused on the New Testament Gospels and the theology of the Apostle Paul.

WORKS CITED

WORKS CITED

Adam, A.K.M. Review of *The New Testament and the People of God*, by Nicholas Thomas Wright. Catholic Biblical Quarterly 56 (1994): 164-166.

Barclay, John. *Paul and the Gift*. Grand Rapids, Mich.: Eerdmans, 2015.

Bartholomew, Gilbert. Review of *The New Testament and the People of God*, by Nicholas Thomas Wright. Homiletic 19:2 (1994): 21-23.

Blomberg, Craig. Review of *The New Testament and the People of God*, by Nicholas Thomas Wright. Criswell Theological Review 7 (1993): 124-126.

Campbell, Douglas. *The Deliverance of God: An Apocalyptic Rereading of Paul*. Grand Rapids, Mich.: Eerdmans, 2009.

Cara, Robert. *Cracking the Foundation of the New Perspective on Paul*. Fearn, U.K.: Christian Focus Publications, 2017.

Cross, Anthony. Review of *The New Testament and the People of God*, by Nicholas Thomas Wright. Journal for the Study of the New Testament 53 (1994): 126.

Dunn, James. *The New Perspective on Paul*. Grand Rapids, Mich.: Eerdmans, 2007.

Gathercole, Simon. *Where is Boasting?: Early Jewish Soteriology and Paul's Response in Romans 1–5*. Grand Rapids, Mich.: Eerdmans, 2002.

Hafemann, Scott. Review of *The New Testament and the People of God*, by Nicholas Thomas Wright. *Journal of the Evangelical Theological Society* 40, no. 2 (1997): 305–8.

Johnson, Luke Timothy. Review of *The New Testament and the People of God*, by Nicholas Thomas Wright. *Journal of Biblical Literature* 113, no. 3 (1994).

Kandiah, Krish. "Three Books That Changed NT Wright's Life." *Christianity Today*. Accessed January 2, 2018. https://www.christiantoday.com/article/three-books-that-changed-nt-wrights-life/104297.htm

Kruse, Colin. *Paul, the Law, and Justification*. Eugene, Oreg.: Wipf & Stock, 2008.

Lewis, C.S. *The Chronicles of Narnia*. New York: Harper Collins, 1956.

Mere Christianity. New York: Harper Collins, 1952.

The Screwtape Letters. London: Geoffrey Bless, 1942.

Meyer, Ben. *Critical Realism and the New Testament*. Princeton Theological Monograph Series, Vol. 17. Alison Park, PA.: Pickwick Publications, 1989.

Piper, John. *The Future of Justification: A Response to N. T. Wright*. Nottingham: Inter-Varsity Press, 2008.

Roberts, Alastair. "N. T. Wright: A Biography." *Alastair's Adversaria*. Accessed January 18, 2018. https://alastairadversaria.com/2006/09/11/nt-wright-a-biography/

Saldarini, Anthony and James VanderKam, *Pharisees, Scribes and Sadducees in Palestinian Society*. Grand Rapids, MI.: Eerdmans, 2001.

Sanders, E.P. *Paul and Palestinian Judaism: A Comparison of Patterns of Religion*. Minneapolis, Minn.: Fortress Press, 1977.

Paul: The Apostle's Life, Letters, and Thought. Minneapolis, Minn.: Fortress Press, 2015.

Paul, the Law, and the Jewish People. Minneapolis, Minn.: Fortress Press, 1983.

Seifrid, Mark. *Christ, Our Righteousness: Paul's Theology of Justification*. Downers Grove, Il.: IVP Academic, 2001.

Stendahl, Krister. "The Apostle Paul and the Introspective Conscience of the West." *Harvard Theological Review* 56, no. 3 (1963).

Stuhlmacher, Peter. *Revisiting Paul's Doctrine of Justification: A Challenge to the New Perspective*. Downers Grove, Il.: IVP Academic, 2001.

VanLandingham, Chris. *Judgment and Justification in Early Judaism and the Apostle Paul*. Grand Rapids, Mich.: Baker Academic, 2006.

Waters, Guy. *Justification and the New Perspectives on Paul: A Review and Response*. Phillipsburg, NJ: P&R Publishing, 2004.

Westerholm, Stephen. *Justification Reconsidered: Rethinking a Pauline Theme*. Grand Rapids, Mich.: Eerdmans, 2013.

Wright, N. T. *The Climax of the Covenant: Christ and the Law in Pauline Theology*. Minneapolis, Minn.: Fortress Press, 1991.

Jesus and the Victory of God. Minneapolis, Minn.: Fortress Press, 1997.

Justification. Grand Rapids, Mich.: IVP Academic, 2009.

The New Testament and the People of God. Minneapolis, Minn.: Fortress Press, 1992.

Paul and the Faithfulness of God. Minneapolis, Minn.: Fortress Press, 2013.

Paul: Fresh Perspectives. Minneapolis, Minn.: Fortress Press, 2005.

The Resurrection of the Son of God. Minneapolis, Minn.: Fortress Press, 2003.

What St Paul Really Said. Grand Rapids, Mich.: Eerdmans, 1997.

THE MACAT LIBRARY
BY DISCIPLINE

AFRICANA STUDIES

Chinua Achebe's *An Image of Africa: Racism in Conrad's Heart of Darkness*
W. E. B. Du Bois's *The Souls of Black Folk*
Zora Neale Huston's *Characteristics of Negro Expression*
Martin Luther King Jr's *Why We Can't Wait*
Toni Morrison's *Playing in the Dark: Whiteness in the American Literary Imagination*

ANTHROPOLOGY

Arjun Appadurai's *Modernity at Large: Cultural Dimensions of Globalisation*
Philippe Ariès's *Centuries of Childhood*
Franz Boas's *Race, Language and Culture*
Kim Chan & Renée Mauborgne's *Blue Ocean Strategy*
Jared Diamond's *Guns, Germs & Steel: the Fate of Human Societies*
Jared Diamond's *Collapse: How Societies Choose to Fail or Survive*
E. E. Evans-Pritchard's *Witchcraft, Oracles and Magic Among the Azande*
James Ferguson's *The Anti-Politics Machine*
Clifford Geertz's *The Interpretation of Cultures*
David Graeber's *Debt: the First 5000 Years*
Karen Ho's *Liquidated: An Ethnography of Wall Street*
Geert Hofstede's *Culture's Consequences: Comparing Values, Behaviors, Institutes and Organizations across Nations*
Claude Lévi-Strauss's *Structural Anthropology*
Jay Macleod's *Ain't No Makin' It: Aspirations and Attainment in a Low-Income Neighborhood*
Saba Mahmood's *The Politics of Piety: The Islamic Revival and the Feminist Subjec*t
Marcel Mauss's *The Gift*

BUSINESS

Jean Lave & Etienne Wenger's *Situated Learning*
Theodore Levitt's *Marketing Myopia*
Burton G. Malkiel's *A Random Walk Down Wall Street*
Douglas McGregor's *The Human Side of Enterprise*
Michael Porter's *Competitive Strategy: Creating and Sustaining Superior Performance*
John Kotter's *Leading Change*
C. K. Prahalad & Gary Hamel's *The Core Competence of the Corporation*

CRIMINOLOGY

Michelle Alexander's *The New Jim Crow: Mass Incarceration in the Age of Colorblindness*
Michael R. Gottfredson & Travis Hirschi's *A General Theory of Crime*
Richard Herrnstein & Charles A. Murray's *The Bell Curve: Intelligence and Class Structure in American Life*
Elizabeth Loftus's *Eyewitness Testimony*
Jay Macleod's *Ain't No Makin' It: Aspirations and Attainment in a Low-Income Neighborhood*
Philip Zimbardo's *The Lucifer Effect*

ECONOMICS

Janet Abu-Lughod's *Before European Hegemony*
Ha-Joon Chang's *Kicking Away the Ladder*
David Brion Davis's *The Problem of Slavery in the Age of Revolution*
Milton Friedman's *The Role of Monetary Policy*
Milton Friedman's *Capitalism and Freedom*
David Graeber's *Debt: the First 5000 Years*
Friedrich Hayek's *The Road to Serfdom*
Karen Ho's *Liquidated: An Ethnography of Wall Street*

John Maynard Keynes's *The General Theory of Employment, Interest and Money*
Charles P. Kindleberger's *Manias, Panics and Crashes*
Robert Lucas's *Why Doesn't Capital Flow from Rich to Poor Countries?*
Burton G. Malkiel's *A Random Walk Down Wall Street*
Thomas Robert Malthus's *An Essay on the Principle of Population*
Karl Marx's *Capital*
Thomas Piketty's *Capital in the Twenty-First Century*
Amartya Sen's *Development as Freedom*
Adam Smith's *The Wealth of Nations*
Nassim Nicholas Taleb's *The Black Swan: The Impact of the Highly Improbable*
Amos Tversky's & Daniel Kahneman's *Judgment under Uncertainty: Heuristics and Biases*
Mahbub Ul Haq's *Reflections on Human Development*
Max Weber's *The Protestant Ethic and the Spirit of Capitalism*

FEMINISM AND GENDER STUDIES

Judith Butler's *Gender Trouble*
Simone De Beauvoir's *The Second Sex*
Michel Foucault's *History of Sexuality*
Betty Friedan's *The Feminine Mystique*
Saba Mahmood's *The Politics of Piety: The Islamic Revival and the Feminist Subjec*t
Joan Wallach Scott's *Gender and the Politics of History*
Mary Wollstonecraft's *A Vindication of the Rights of Woman*
Virginia Woolf's *A Room of One's Own*

GEOGRAPHY

The Brundtland Report's *Our Common Future*
Rachel Carson's *Silent Spring*
Charles Darwin's *On the Origin of Species*
James Ferguson's *The Anti-Politics Machine*
Jane Jacobs's *The Death and Life of Great American Cities*
James Lovelock's *Gaia: A New Look at Life on Earth*
Amartya Sen's *Development as Freedom*
Mathis Wackernagel & William Rees's *Our Ecological Footprint*

HISTORY

Janet Abu-Lughod's *Before European Hegemony*
Benedict Anderson's *Imagined Communities*
Bernard Bailyn's *The Ideological Origins of the American Revolution*
Hanna Batatu's *The Old Social Classes And The Revolutionary Movements Of Iraq*
Christopher Browning's *Ordinary Men: Reserve Police Batallion 101 and the Final Solution in Poland*
Edmund Burke's *Reflections on the Revolution in France*
William Cronon's *Nature's Metropolis: Chicago And The Great West*
Alfred W. Crosby's *The Columbian Exchange*
Hamid Dabashi's *Iran: A People Interrupted*
David Brion Davis's *The Problem of Slavery in the Age of Revolution*
Nathalie Zemon Davis's *The Return of Martin Guerre*
Jared Diamond's *Guns, Germs & Steel: the Fate of Human Societies*
Frank Dikotter's *Mao's Great Famine*
John W Dower's *War Without Mercy: Race And Power In The Pacific War*
W. E. B. Du Bois's *The Souls of Black Folk*
Richard J. Evans's *In Defence of History*
Lucien Febvre's *The Problem of Unbelief in the 16th Century*
Sheila Fitzpatrick's *Everyday Stalinism*

Eric Foner's *Reconstruction: America's Unfinished Revolution, 1863-1877*
Michel Foucault's *Discipline and Punish*
Michel Foucault's *History of Sexuality*
Francis Fukuyama's *The End of History and the Last Man*
John Lewis Gaddis's *We Now Know: Rethinking Cold War History*
Ernest Gellner's *Nations and Nationalism*
Eugene Genovese's *Roll, Jordan, Roll: The World the Slaves Made*
Carlo Ginzburg's *The Night Battles*
Daniel Goldhagen's *Hitler's Willing Executioners*
Jack Goldstone's *Revolution and Rebellion in the Early Modern World*
Antonio Gramsci's *The Prison Notebooks*
Alexander Hamilton, John Jay & James Madison's *The Federalist Papers*
Christopher Hill's *The World Turned Upside Down*
Carole Hillenbrand's *The Crusades: Islamic Perspectives*
Thomas Hobbes's *Leviathan*
Eric Hobsbawm's *The Age Of Revolution*
John A. Hobson's *Imperialism: A Study*
Albert Hourani's *History of the Arab Peoples*
Samuel P. Huntington's *The Clash of Civilizations and the Remaking of World Order*
C. L. R. James's *The Black Jacobins*
Tony Judt's *Postwar: A History of Europe Since 1945*
Ernst Kantorowicz's *The King's Two Bodies: A Study in Medieval Political Theology*
Paul Kennedy's *The Rise and Fall of the Great Powers*
Ian Kershaw's *The "Hitler Myth": Image and Reality in the Third Reich*
John Maynard Keynes's *The General Theory of Employment, Interest and Money*
Charles P. Kindleberger's *Manias, Panics and Crashes*
Martin Luther King Jr's *Why We Can't Wait*
Henry Kissinger's *World Order: Reflections on the Character of Nations and the Course of History*
Thomas Kuhn's *The Structure of Scientific Revolutions*
Georges Lefebvre's *The Coming of the French Revolution*
John Locke's *Two Treatises of Government*
Niccolò Machiavelli's *The Prince*
Thomas Robert Malthus's *An Essay on the Principle of Population*
Mahmood Mamdani's *Citizen and Subject: Contemporary Africa And The Legacy Of Late Colonialism*
Karl Marx's *Capital*
Stanley Milgram's *Obedience to Authority*
John Stuart Mill's *On Liberty*
Thomas Paine's *Common Sense*
Thomas Paine's *Rights of Man*
Geoffrey Parker's *Global Crisis: War, Climate Change and Catastrophe in the Seventeenth Century*
Jonathan Riley-Smith's *The First Crusade and the Idea of Crusading*
Jean-Jacques Rousseau's *The Social Contract*
Joan Wallach Scott's *Gender and the Politics of History*
Theda Skocpol's *States and Social Revolutions*
Adam Smith's *The Wealth of Nations*
Timothy Snyder's *Bloodlands: Europe Between Hitler and Stalin*
Sun Tzu's *The Art of War*
Keith Thomas's *Religion and the Decline of Magic*
Thucydides's *The History of the Peloponnesian War*
Frederick Jackson Turner's *The Significance of the Frontier in American History*
Odd Arne Westad's *The Global Cold War: Third World Interventions And The Making Of Our Times*

LITERATURE

Chinua Achebe's *An Image of Africa: Racism in Conrad's Heart of Darkness*
Roland Barthes's *Mythologies*
Homi K. Bhabha's *The Location of Culture*
Judith Butler's *Gender Trouble*
Simone De Beauvoir's *The Second Sex*
Ferdinand De Saussure's *Course in General Linguistics*
T. S. Eliot's *The Sacred Wood: Essays on Poetry and Criticism*
Zora Neale Huston's *Characteristics of Negro Expression*
Toni Morrison's *Playing in the Dark: Whiteness in the American Literary Imagination*
Edward Said's *Orientalism*
Gayatri Chakravorty Spivak's *Can the Subaltern Speak?*
Mary Wollstonecraft's *A Vindication of the Rights of Women*
Virginia Woolf's *A Room of One's Own*

PHILOSOPHY

Elizabeth Anscombe's *Modern Moral Philosophy*
Hannah Arendt's *The Human Condition*
Aristotle's *Metaphysics*
Aristotle's *Nicomachean Ethics*
Edmund Gettier's *Is Justified True Belief Knowledge?*
Georg Wilhelm Friedrich Hegel's *Phenomenology of Spirit*
David Hume's *Dialogues Concerning Natural Religion*
David Hume's *The Enquiry for Human Understanding*
Immanuel Kant's *Religion within the Boundaries of Mere Reason*
Immanuel Kant's *Critique of Pure Reason*
Søren Kierkegaard's *The Sickness Unto Death*
Søren Kierkegaard's *Fear and Trembling*
C. S. Lewis's *The Abolition of Man*
Alasdair MacIntyre's *After Virtue*
Marcus Aurelius's *Meditations*
Friedrich Nietzsche's *On the Genealogy of Morality*
Friedrich Nietzsche's *Beyond Good and Evil*
Plato's *Republic*
Plato's *Symposium*
Jean-Jacques Rousseau's *The Social Contract*
Gilbert Ryle's *The Concept of Mind*
Baruch Spinoza's *Ethics*
Sun Tzu's *The Art of War*
Ludwig Wittgenstein's *Philosophical Investigations*

POLITICS

Benedict Anderson's *Imagined Communities*
Aristotle's *Politics*
Bernard Bailyn's *The Ideological Origins of the American Revolution*
Edmund Burke's *Reflections on the Revolution in France*
John C. Calhoun's *A Disquisition on Government*
Ha-Joon Chang's *Kicking Away the Ladder*
Hamid Dabashi's *Iran: A People Interrupted*
Hamid Dabashi's *Theology of Discontent: The Ideological Foundation of the Islamic Revolution in Iran*
Robert Dahl's *Democracy and its Critics*
Robert Dahl's *Who Governs?*
David Brion Davis's *The Problem of Slavery in the Age of Revolution*

Alexis De Tocqueville's *Democracy in America*
James Ferguson's *The Anti-Politics Machine*
Frank Dikotter's *Mao's Great Famine*
Sheila Fitzpatrick's *Everyday Stalinism*
Eric Foner's *Reconstruction: America's Unfinished Revolution, 1863-1877*
Milton Friedman's *Capitalism and Freedom*
Francis Fukuyama's *The End of History and the Last Man*
John Lewis Gaddis's *We Now Know: Rethinking Cold War History*
Ernest Gellner's *Nations and Nationalism*
David Graeber's *Debt: the First 5000 Years*
Antonio Gramsci's *The Prison Notebooks*
Alexander Hamilton, John Jay & James Madison's *The Federalist Papers*
Friedrich Hayek's *The Road to Serfdom*
Christopher Hill's *The World Turned Upside Down*
Thomas Hobbes's *Leviathan*
John A. Hobson's *Imperialism: A Study*
Samuel P. Huntington's *The Clash of Civilizations and the Remaking of World Order*
Tony Judt's *Postwar: A History of Europe Since 1945*
David C. Kang's *China Rising: Peace, Power and Order in East Asia*
Paul Kennedy's *The Rise and Fall of Great Powers*
Robert Keohane's *After Hegemony*
Martin Luther King Jr.'s *Why We Can't Wait*
Henry Kissinger's *World Order: Reflections on the Character of Nations and the Course of History*
John Locke's *Two Treatises of Government*
Niccolò Machiavelli's *The Prince*
Thomas Robert Malthus's *An Essay on the Principle of Population*
Mahmood Mamdani's *Citizen and Subject: Contemporary Africa And The Legacy Of Late Colonialism*
Karl Marx's *Capital*
John Stuart Mill's *On Liberty*
John Stuart Mill's *Utilitarianism*
Hans Morgenthau's *Politics Among Nations*
Thomas Paine's *Common Sense*
Thomas Paine's *Rights of Man*
Thomas Piketty's *Capital in the Twenty-First Century*
Robert D. Putman's *Bowling Alone*
John Rawls's *Theory of Justice*
Jean-Jacques Rousseau's *The Social Contract*
Theda Skocpol's *States and Social Revolutions*
Adam Smith's *The Wealth of Nations*
Sun Tzu's *The Art of War*
Henry David Thoreau's *Civil Disobedience*
Thucydides's *The History of the Peloponnesian War*
Kenneth Waltz's *Theory of International Politics*
Max Weber's *Politics as a Vocation*
Odd Arne Westad's *The Global Cold War: Third World Interventions And The Making Of Our Times*

POSTCOLONIAL STUDIES

Roland Barthes's *Mythologies*
Frantz Fanon's *Black Skin, White Masks*
Homi K. Bhabha's *The Location of Culture*
Gustavo Gutiérrez's *A Theology of Liberation*
Edward Said's *Orientalism*
Gayatri Chakravorty Spivak's *Can the Subaltern Speak?*

PSYCHOLOGY

Gordon Allport's *The Nature of Prejudice*
Alan Baddeley & Graham Hitch's *Aggression: A Social Learning Analysis*
Albert Bandura's *Aggression: A Social Learning Analysis*
Leon Festinger's *A Theory of Cognitive Dissonance*
Sigmund Freud's *The Interpretation of Dreams*
Betty Friedan's *The Feminine Mystique*
Michael R. Gottfredson & Travis Hirschi's *A General Theory of Crime*
Eric Hoffer's *The True Believer: Thoughts on the Nature of Mass Movements*
William James's *Principles of Psychology*
Elizabeth Loftus's *Eyewitness Testimony*
A. H. Maslow's *A Theory of Human Motivation*
Stanley Milgram's *Obedience to Authority*
Steven Pinker's *The Better Angels of Our Nature*
Oliver Sacks's *The Man Who Mistook His Wife For a Hat*
Richard Thaler & Cass Sunstein's *Nudge: Improving Decisions About Health, Wealth and Happiness*
Amos Tversky's *Judgment under Uncertainty: Heuristics and Biases*
Philip Zimbardo's *The Lucifer Effect*

SCIENCE

Rachel Carson's *Silent Spring*
William Cronon's *Nature's Metropolis: Chicago And The Great West*
Alfred W. Crosby's *The Columbian Exchange*
Charles Darwin's *On the Origin of Species*
Richard Dawkin's *The Selfish Gene*
Thomas Kuhn's *The Structure of Scientific Revolutions*
Geoffrey Parker's *Global Crisis: War, Climate Change and Catastrophe in the Seventeenth Century*
Mathis Wackernagel & William Rees's *Our Ecological Footprint*

SOCIOLOGY

Michelle Alexander's *The New Jim Crow: Mass Incarceration in the Age of Colorblindness*
Gordon Allport's *The Nature of Prejudice*
Albert Bandura's *Aggression: A Social Learning Analysis*
Hanna Batatu's *The Old Social Classes And The Revolutionary Movements Of Iraq*
Ha-Joon Chang's *Kicking Away the Ladder*
W. E. B. Du Bois's *The Souls of Black Folk*
Émile Durkheim's *On Suicide*
Frantz Fanon's *Black Skin, White Masks*
Frantz Fanon's *The Wretched of the Earth*
Eric Foner's *Reconstruction: America's Unfinished Revolution, 1863-1877*
Eugene Genovese's *Roll, Jordan, Roll: The World the Slaves Made*
Jack Goldstone's *Revolution and Rebellion in the Early Modern World*
Antonio Gramsci's *The Prison Notebooks*
Richard Herrnstein & Charles A Murray's *The Bell Curve: Intelligence and Class Structure in American Life*
Eric Hoffer's *The True Believer: Thoughts on the Nature of Mass Movements*
Jane Jacobs's *The Death and Life of Great American Cities*
Robert Lucas's *Why Doesn't Capital Flow from Rich to Poor Countries?*
Jay Macleod's *Ain't No Makin' It: Aspirations and Attainment in a Low Income Neighborhood*
Elaine May's *Homeward Bound: American Families in the Cold War Era*
Douglas McGregor's *The Human Side of Enterprise*
C. Wright Mills's *The Sociological Imagination*

Thomas Piketty's *Capital in the Twenty-First Century*
Robert D. Putman's *Bowling Alone*
David Riesman's *The Lonely Crowd: A Study of the Changing American Character*
Edward Said's *Orientalism*
Joan Wallach Scott's *Gender and the Politics of History*
Theda Skocpol's *States and Social Revolutions*
Max Weber's *The Protestant Ethic and the Spirit of Capitalism*

THEOLOGY

Augustine's *Confessions*
Benedict's *Rule of St Benedict*
Gustavo Gutiérrez's *A Theology of Liberation*
Carole Hillenbrand's *The Crusades: Islamic Perspectives*
David Hume's *Dialogues Concerning Natural Religion*
Immanuel Kant's *Religion within the Boundaries of Mere Reason*
Ernst Kantorowicz's *The King's Two Bodies: A Study in Medieval Political Theology*
Søren Kierkegaard's *The Sickness Unto Death*
C. S. Lewis's *The Abolition of Man*
Saba Mahmood's *The Politics of Piety: The Islamic Revival and the Feminist Subject*
Baruch Spinoza's *Ethics*
Keith Thomas's *Religion and the Decline of Magic*

Macat Disciplines

Access the greatest ideas and thinkers across entire disciplines, including

INEQUALITY

Ha-Joon Chang's, *Kicking Away the Ladder*

David Graeber's, *Debt: The First 5000 Years*

Robert E. Lucas's, *Why Doesn't Capital Flow from Rich To Poor Countries?*

Thomas Piketty's, *Capital in the Twenty-First Century*

Amartya Sen's, *Inequality Re-Examined*

Mahbub Ul Haq's, *Reflections on Human Development*

Macat analyses are available from all good bookshops and libraries.

Access hundreds of analyses through one, multimedia tool.
Join free for one month **library.macat.com**

Macat Disciplines

Access the greatest ideas and thinkers across entire disciplines, including

CRIMINOLOGY

Michelle Alexander's
*The New Jim Crow:
Mass Incarceration in the
Age of Colorblindness*

**Michael R. Gottfredson
& Travis Hirschi's**
A General Theory of Crime

Elizabeth Loftus's
Eyewitness Testimony

**Richard Herrnstein
& Charles A. Murray's**
*The Bell Curve: Intelligence and
Class Structure in American Life*

Jay Macleod's
*Ain't No Makin' It:
Aspirations and Attainment in a
Low-Income Neighborhood*

Philip Zimbardo's
The Lucifer Effect

Macat analyses are available from all good bookshops and libraries.

Access hundreds of analyses through one, multimedia tool.
Join free for one month **library.macat.com**

Macat Disciplines

Access the greatest ideas and thinkers across entire disciplines, including

Postcolonial Studies

Roland Barthes's *Mythologies*
Frantz Fanon's *Black Skin, White Masks*
Homi K. Bhabha's *The Location of Culture*
Gustavo Gutiérrez's *A Theology of Liberation*
Edward Said's *Orientalism*
Gayatri Chakravorty Spivak's *Can the Subaltern Speak?*

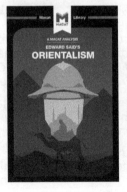

Macat analyses are available from all good bookshops and libraries.

Access hundreds of analyses through one, multimedia tool.
Join free for one month **library.macat.com**